The Great Reset
And its Health Dictatorship

Threefold Publishing

The Great Reset

And its Health Dictatorship

A Guide to Freedom in the Post-Corona World

First English edition
© 2021 Threefold Publishing

Threefold Publishing
P.O. Box 251
Mountlake Terrace, WA 98043
www.cfae.us/threefold-publishing

Financial support for the English edition was generously donated by Dr. Sigrid
Penrod, ND.

Originally published in Dutch by Nearchus, Assen as De Grote Reset, 2021
German publication by Edition Immanente, Berlin as Der Grosse Reset, 2021

English Translation: Harrie Salman
English Edition Editor: Ed Conroy
English Edition Cover Design: Ulja Novatschkova, Berlin
Cover Images: janjf93 (pixabay) and kimberrywood (istockphoto)

A CIP record for this book is available from the Library of Congress Cataloging-
in-Publication Data

ISBN 978-1-7363165-1-1

Printed and bound in United States of America

Contents

FEAR EATS THE SOUL

In Bulgaria, a story is told of a king who was travelling to his capital. Along the way, he took an old woman with him on his horse, who said she also wanted to go there. When the king asked the old woman why she was also going to the city, she replied that she was the plague and that she had come to take 300 people from the city. After they arrived in the capital and parted ways, a plague did indeed strike the inhabitants of the city. Once the plague had subsided, the king received a report that more than 1,000 people ultimately died of the plague. The king sent for the woman and asked her why she had taken more people than she had originally declared to him. She replied that the more than 700 other people had died from their fear of the plague.

Preface to the American Edition

By Ed Conroy

This little book, if its contents were absorbed by a critical mass of people of good will, could provide the basis for some truly transformational conversations that might heal our society's polarization—and help us retain our humanity and freedom.

Its author, Harrie Salman, was born in Noordwijk, Holland, in 1953. He is very much a European scholar, researcher, and writer, having earned his doctorate in the philosophy of education from Prague University in the Czech Republic. He makes his home in The Netherlands and lectures widely in many countries. With fluency in seven Western European languages plus Russian and several Eastern European languages, he is also a social scientist, a keen student of the extraordinary changes that have taken place in Europe since the fall of the Soviet Union.

Harrie is also a sharp observer of life in the United States, and in particular of our responses, official and unofficial, to what he appropriately calls "the Corona crisis."

Most significantly, Harrie is a philosopher in the very traditional sense of being a "lover of wisdom." In the course of his life, he has made a deep study of not only rationalist philosophy but also Western esoteric spiritual traditions, particularly as expressed in the last century by the Austrian scholar and mystic Rudolf Steiner, founder of the Anthroposophical movement. As the author of books with such titles as "The Social World As Mystery Center: The Social Vision of Anthroposophy" and "Europe: A Continent with a Global Mission," it is evident that Harrie has taken on the job of being a re-interpreter of that tradition, and of Anthroposophic perspectives, for new generations of readers.

For American readers, it is fair to say, the once towering figure of Rudolf Steiner is associated more with his capsule biography in Wikipedia than with his uniquely powerful presence as a force for social reform in post-World War I Europe. Nor is Steiner widely known in the United States for his lasting contributions to education, medicine and agriculture, and his contributions to understanding the place of humanity both in our world and our cosmos.

We are fortunate that Harrie has taken on the job of re-animating Rudolf Steiner's thought and is proving himself equal to its demands.

This new and admittedly compact book by Harrie Salman, although its subject matter may not immediately appear to relate to the Western mystery traditions, is most definitely an expression of the energies that charge that philosophical current in Harrie's writing career. It is, in the best sense of the word, a manifesto, in which he analyzes the ills of our times, calls out those persons and institutions he sees as responsible for those ills, and issues a call to action. He addresses that call to action to all of us who believe that individuals and groups working together can renew and liberate our society. He calls on us to become fully human and enrich our social lives—impoverished by the lockdowns of what he calls "the health dictatorship"—from the bottom up, with inspiration from the Divine. It is a noble call, and Harrie is quite aware that the tasks he outlines will not be easily accomplished.

The suggestions for personal and social reform Harrie makes at the conclusion of this book show that he is not only a lover of wisdom, but very much a lover of human beings, of humanity as a whole, and of all that it means to be human. At one time, prior to the advent of the Fourth Industrial Revolution, a concept Harrie explains in some detail, it might have been considered a rather bland statement to say that someone such as Harrie is a "lover of humanity."

As an example of how the concept of "humanity" has been relegated to irrelevance in popular culture, I recall the character of the washed-up Hollywood screenwriter Steven Philips well-played by Albert Brooks in the 1999 film, "The Muse." The film begins with Philips receiving an "Humanitarian of the Year" award at a gala dinner. He regards such public recognition as an "humanitarian" not as an honor but as tangible proof of his obsolescence as far as the film industry is concerned, not worth a dime to his career.

Today, however, in the Year of Our Lord 2021, to take a stand for humanity is nothing less than a radical act of rebellion, of defiance, against a veritable *blitzkrieg* of dehumanizing technologies that are assaulting all human beings—in body, soul, mind and, most of all, spirit. From synthetic biology to geoengineering to universal covert and overt surveillance of everyone and everything, we human beings, all around the globe, are moving, like it or not, into a very Brave New World.

In this manifesto, Harrie asserts that the COVID-19 epidemic—which he refuses to call a "pandemic" for reasons he explains in detail—was expected and prepared for by a wide range of experts from business, institutional medicine, pharmaceutical companies, the World Health Organization, Big Tech companies and others. Moreover, as Peter McCullough, MD and others have pointed out, they assured that this expected epidemic would become dangerous by discouraging prehospital treatment and by prohibiting the use of certain inexpensive, well-established, and effective drugs.

The Big Tech companies assisted this effort by a massive censorship campaign across all mainstream platforms. Anonymous "fact checkers" assisted in the work of deleting from the internet all messages with online guidance from holistic doctors and other health practitioners to the effect that people could increase their natural immunity and lessen the severity of a case of COVID-19 by taking Vitamin D, Vitamin C, Zinc, and other supplements, and all messages critical of vaccines.

This group of people who anticipated and prepared for the epidemic, Harrie further asserts, orchestrated their global, digitally coordinated management of this health crisis as a means of frightening the people of the world into taking the new so-called "vaccines." Harrie further asserts that the campaign for the vaccination of everyone on earth publicly advocated by Bill Gates, the agencies he funds and world leaders echoing that message constitutes the first step toward the institution of a global, technocratic dictatorship under the cover of the worldwide COVID-19 "health emergency."

Such a dictatorship—to be gently imposed in the ostensibly "humanitarian" interest of presumably saving the people of the world from a collapsing ecosphere—has long been discussed by the leading luminaries who participate in the World Economic Forum. Until the world-wide lockdowns imposed in line with the WHO's mandates, when the world came to a standstill with disastrous economic consequences for millions of people, I, for one, did not take such talk seriously.

Such an attitude is still prevalent among many people who consider themselves well informed on the basis of their diet of information from mainstream media sources, where nary a pundit dares raise serious questions about the vast changes in every aspect of society and nature itself being marketed under the new brand of "The Great Reset."

I am a former investigative reporter, however, and I like to look behind the curtain in the hope of perhaps finding evidence of one or more charlatans posing as the "Great and Powerful Oz," pulling the levers that control the smoke and mirrors that distract the people from their machinations. During the past year, just like millions of other people, I have conducted my own research into the origins and dynamics of the Coronavirus, in the company of like-minded friends who have pointed me to new information by some brilliant independent researchers ignored by the mainstream media. As a result of my own research into such information, I am seeing certain patterns of deception beneath the façade of a global "pandemic." So, too, have numerous other people seen patterns of deception. Many tens of thousands, perhaps millions of them have participated in massive, mis-reported public protests around the world against the lockdowns and the dominant Corona narrative.

As Harrie so thoroughly illustrates in this book, we are now at the point where we can easily see that support for the vast transformations of the Great Reset is being expressed quite seriously and earnestly by leaders of the world's greatest nations. They have clearly made so much progress in laying down the infrastructure for the changes they envision that they are confident they can announce their intentions with impunity. They are joined by the leaders of the major foundations, major media organizations, and others in the NGOs, academic institutions and marketing and public relations firms who have decided it is in their interest to become aligned with the values and agendas of global rule by technocrats. They are busily spreading their message, even enlisting such beloved television personalities and lovers of the natural world as David Attenborough to advocate in a Netflix "documentary" for their technocratic approach to saving nature by demanding it come under complete control.

I have no doubt many of those leaders consider themselves people of good will who sincerely believe that their way, which includes a complete transformation in every sphere of economic, cultural, and political life in the presumed interest of "sustainability," is "the only way" to "save humanity." There is no doubt that all of nature is in crisis—including all of humanity, of course. As someone who participated in environmental activism in the 1970s and 1980s, I must observe that the very term "sustainability" has become hijacked by technocratic thinking and bears no relationship to its earlier definition in the original environmental movement.

"Sustainability" now implies the imposition of a global surveillance and measuring system for the control of all of nature, from agricultural production to water levels in wells on private property, so that all "inputs" and "outputs" may be centrally monitored and regulated by technocrats mining information from a vast database in "the Cloud." It includes a massive, well-intentioned, but misinformed campaign to "reduce greenhouse gas emissions," as they are now considered by mainstream environmental scientists, environmental activists, and their partners in a new "green energy industry" the primary threat to the survival of nature and humanity. Other issues such as air and water pollution are relegated to secondary importance. Moreover, the longstanding, massive, global release of toxic substances and nanoparticles into the atmosphere via covert geoengineering programs—which J. Marvin Herndon, Ph.D. asserts do more to contribute to global warming than greenhouse gases—is misrepresented in the media and excluded from mainstream public policy debates regarding global warming.

"Sustainability" therefore no longer refers to the earlier environmentalist concept of working to create advances in science, legislation, public behavior, and regulations intended to return the highly damaged and polluted natural world and all its creatures—including humanity—to a healthier condition in which nature may become once again *self-sustaining* and *self-regulating*, as it was of course for many millions of years before the advent of the Fourth Industrial Revolution.

Through the World Economic Forum and other means, the advocates of this presumably altruistic effort to save humanity and nature have invested millions of dollars and euros in very sophisticated public relations campaigns, even getting a cover story on the Great Reset in *Time Magazine*. They clearly mean business, and they see this current crisis as a great business opportunity.

Harrie gives us the historical context for this movement, tracing its origins back to its progenitor in the Technocracy organization that grew out of a group of social engineers at Columbia University in the 1930s. He points out that technocratic ideas got a foothold in the US under the New Deal, and it goes without saying that both Nazi Germany and the Soviet Union under Stalin embraced centralized planning—with disastrous results.

Harrie Salman is not the first author, of course, to make such a bold assertion linking the official response to SARS-CoV-2 to the risk of global totalitarianism. He is in very good company with numerous other outspoken critics, researchers and public educators who have, in their own ways, made similar arguments. Such persons include Dr. Joseph Mercola, Ronnie Cummins, Naomi Wolf, Robert F. Kennedy, Jr., Dr. Kelly Brogan and her husband Sayer Ji, Dr. Christianne Northrup, Alison McDowell, Whitney Webb, Dr. Peter Breggin and Gina Breggin, Dr. Dolores Cahill, Dr. Sherri Tenpenny, among many other authors, educators and researchers who have all, to differing degrees, experienced significant online censorship of their work.

If what these highly educated and experienced professionals—some of whom used to be lionized in the mass media to great popular acclaim—have to say is so very much in error, as

claimed by the censors in Big Tech, why then bother to de-plat-
form them, de-monetize them, and employ publicists to defame
them? Why would they attack such remarkable women and men
courageous enough to dissent at great cost to themselves, their
careers, and their social standing?

Harrie is the first among these many authors and speakers
that I have seen in my surveys of the extensive literature of protest
against the dominant COVID-19 narrative, however, to directly
link this global crisis to the ideas Rudolf Steiner put forward at
the end of World War I for a "threefold social order." Steiner did
so as an alternative to what seemed to many educated people of
the day as the bankruptcy of traditional capitalism, the rapacious
empires fed by forced labor, and the emerging Communist totalitarian society being seeded in Russia at that time by Vladimir I.
Lenin and the Bolsheviks.

Steiner proposed that societies be reorganized in a manner
that would create three separate institutional spheres in which
authority would be established in economics, organized in
accord with the values of brotherhood and cooperation; culture,
including spirituality and art, organized in accord with the value
of freedom; and politics, encompassing the work of the state and
law, organized in accord with the value of equality.

Although Steiner's initiatives for global social reform,
along with many of his other initiatives, were almost completely
submerged by the rising tide of National Socialism in Germany
and the ensuing Second World War, they are re-emerging in the
work of numerous authors and activists in our times. We are
once again at a point—13 years after the world financial crisis of
2008—in which it is evident that both capitalism and socialism

as they are being practiced in the world at this time via the issue of fiat currencies are morally and politically bankrupt. People are wise to the predatory nature of international business, even when masked as "neoliberalism." Moreover, the number of nations that have already veered into highly authoritarian, centralized, totalitarian governments in which dissident believers, intellectuals, journalists, and others are persecuted, systematically imprisoned and "re-educated" or simply killed by state agents or their friends in organized crime—with complete official impunity—is growing year by year.

How, then, would "social three-folding" work?" Balance is a central concept. According to the anonymous author of the blog at ecalpemos.org: "For society to function healthily the three areas of activity (economics, culture and politics) need to be held in balance. If one dominates then society will not function properly."

I quote this anonymous blogger to illustrate a larger point, which is that the concept of "social three-folding" has come to have a growing presence on the internet. It is an idea advanced by contemporary Anthroposophists such as Stephen E. Usher, Ph.D., who has written with erudition and eloquence on the subject and is dedicated to promoting a wider discussion of it, as well as by others. The leadership of the MysTech organization, allied with the publisher of this book, is also promoting a wider discussion of these matters through its annual online conferences, publications, and other activities.

As the person who worked closely with Harrie in preparing the American edition of this book, I draw attention to his contributions in this area for I think that they provide a very useful framework for thinking about creating meaningful alternatives, in economics, culture and politics, to the technocratic worldview of the Great Reset. Harrie's suggestions at the end of this book represent, in my opinion, seed-ideas that, if properly planted and cared for in the gardens of our minds, could sprout in very meaningful and liberating ways.

There have been a lot of people advocating a wide variety of "meaningful alternatives" in social organization for a very long time, of course, and some of those "alternatives" have produced very strange fruit, indeed. If some of us see evidence the United States is becoming a totally digitized surveillance society, we can easily find others that are far more advanced in that respect than we are, in both Asia and Europe. Even so, it is curious to me that in the United States we are very loath to engage in public debate about the future direction of our democratic republic in relationship to the new technologies of the Fourth Industrial Revolution.

I have no doubt that many thoughtful persons, not only in the United States, but throughout our world, will reject out of hand the idea what they are likely to call the COVID-19 pandemic was anticipated and prepared for by a clique of powerful people. They see the Corona crisis as a genuine global health emergency and regard any attempt to downplay what they regard as the extreme dangerousness of the SARS-CoV-2 virus as a heartless disregard for the real suffering and death the virus has caused. Naomi Klein, highly recognized for her brilliant critique of the predatory behavior of international corporations in her noted book "Disaster Capitalism," has prominently taken such a position. Moreover, she has coined the term, or shall I say epithet, "coronavirus denier," which has resonances with another, very well-known term.

The term "coronavirus denier," I must point out, does not apply accurately to all persons who disagree with the dominant "pandemic" narrative. The dissenters themselves are not in agreement on the question of whether the virus has been proven to exist on the basis of traditional lab assays, whether it emerged naturally or whether it is the result of "gain of function" engineering in a lab.

In addition, we must recognize that many well-educated, reasonable people will likewise reject out of hand the proposition that this current COVID-19 health emergency is a prelude to world technocratic dictatorship because they think that the establishment of such a regime is simply impossible, given the fact that large parts of the world are still without internet access and that indigenous peoples will be resistant to such a regime. Moreover, such people argue, the idea that the world is run by a "cabal" of brilliantly evil people is just a simplistic "conspiracy theory" that ignores the true complexity of our world. Many of them think, moreover, that the atmosphere of fear the authorities promoted during the rollout of the Corona crisis was justifiable. Today, many such people seem to me reluctant to relinquish their fear.

As someone who grew up in the Cold War, when the United States and the Soviet Union steered perilously close to nuclear war in the fall of 1962 during the Cuban Missile Crisis, I know what it is like to live for years with fear. Millions of people in my generation were taught as children that the world could end at any moment from a nuclear strike, and we participated in ridiculous "duck and cover" exercises in our classrooms to "prepare" us for such a strike. As a child, I was deathly afraid I would never grow into adulthood, and that the world would be incinerated. Such fear, in my opinion, traumatized the people in my generation in ways from which we are still endeavoring to heal.

I feel compassion, therefore, for the many people, especially young people, and people with compromised immune systems, who have been terrorized by the official pronouncements about the presumably great dangers of this "novel" virus. Harrie demonstrates very well how such dangers were now verifiably overblown. Even so, there will be many people who will simply reject such information for emotional reasons, or who will never learn of it. I think, therefore, it will take many years for such people, and especially the children who have had to stay at home and take their instruction digitally far away from their friends and playgrounds, to heal from the traumas of the lockdowns.

I hope such younger people will attempt to understand, though, that those of us who grew up under constant terror of the end of the world by nuclear weapons might well be skeptical of the claims of people associated with the WHO, NIH, and CDC that we should submit to a health dictatorship because of the supposed dangers of a microscopic virus, whether it be "novel" or "engineered." Even during the Cold War, no leaders seriously suggested we needed to dispense with our rights to privacy, free speech, and bodily autonomy as guaranteed by the US Constitution because of the dangers of Mutual Assured Destruction by nuclear weapons. Even during the Spanish flu epidemic in 1918, people in the US continued going to work as the idea of the federal government arrogating to itself the power to shut down business across the country was completely unacceptable to the American people.

Here is an irony for us all to consider: A great many people in leadership positions in the US will now readily agree, on the basis of what we have learned about the events that led to the devastating financial crisis of 2008, that there were groups of people in the financial industry who anticipated and prepared for, and indeed benefited massively from that crisis. Why, then, is it now the case that the suggestion that there exists a group of people who anticipated and prepared for the current Corona crisis—and who stand to benefit, particularly in the pharmaceutical industry, from this crisis—utterly dismissed as a reckless "conspiracy theory?"

I hope such people, who include in my case many family members and dear friends, will try to understand the dissenters' skepticism, too, about the presumed health benefits of submitting to injection with insufficiently tested "vaccines" that are producing an alarming number of deaths and adverse reactions among people who have received them—while the pharmaceutical industry remains free of any liability.

On the other hand, skepticism in the face of the sweeping warnings so many people are issuing about imminent technocratic dictatorship is very much justified. There are many claims that need to be tested, much research and public education that needs to be done about the sweeping changes already underway to introduce digital IDs on blockchain, vaccine passports, and move education increasingly into the digital sphere—to mention only a few significant and potentially highly profitable ventures of the Great Reset.

It would be wonderful if our legislative bodies and intellectual leaders would strike up genuine, well-informed public debate about such matters. True debate, however, is hampered by censorship of dissent and the very unfortunate fact that it appears that intellectual leaders of our country at universities, colleges, and medical schools have in general refused to open their campuses to a spirit of free inquiry and debate about the Coronavirus. They have not encouraged students to exercise their critical thinking skills and question the official science justifying the lockdowns and the corresponding policies put in place by health and governmental authorities. There is some indication such inquiry and debate are beginning in the US Congress and in state legislatures, though, and that is an encouraging development.

As someone who participated in protests against the Viet Nam War in high school and college, I distinctly remember that very few educated young people believed the official pronouncements of the federal government regarding that war. The publication in *The New York Times* and *The Washington Post* of "The Pentagon Papers," courageously leaked by Daniel Ellsberg, proved us right. "Teach-ins" were organized on campuses across the country to provide students with an education on the history of Indochina and the nature of its peoples' conflicts with the French and the US and framed the war in terms of colonialism and imperialism, because such information was not generally provided in the standard classroom curricula of the day.

Where, then, are the brave young professors and students who might lead "teach-ins" about the "war on the Coronavirus," as it has been called by Bill Gates and others, and frame it as a new project of technocratic imperialism? Where are the medical students who are demanding to know more about alternative treatments for COVID-19 that have been officially prohibited and misrepresented in the media? Where are the distinguished leaders of major hospitals who might be clamoring to investigate such alternative treatments so as to make them more available? I wonder, indeed, where they are.

We are living in times in which an ideological orthodoxy about the Coronavirus has become well established among educated people who choose to believe that the original pronouncements about the dangerousness of the virus and the presumed powerlessness of our immune systems against it, plus the lockdown measures, etc., were and remain appropriate. While the people who formulate this orthodoxy are willing to question the motives of people in almost every other industry, for some reason the medical establishment and their allies in the pharmaceutical industry have remained sacrosanct, untouchable. Those who disagree with this belief system on the basis of their own rational inquiries, and their studies of suppressed scientific information and clinical practices, have become regarded as heretics by people in positions of authority, power, and influence.

It is indeed a belief system, for the mainstream media have failed to give "fair and balanced" coverage to both sides in this conflict, making it very difficult to obtain *verifiable knowledge* such as Harrie provides in this book. Such dissenters from orthodox beliefs about the virus and the lockdowns are suffering all the stigmatization and social rejection heretics have experienced in every age. Some are even hearing themselves accused by intolerant colleagues, as one friend related to me, of having been "brainwashed," a very strong term. We can at least be thankful the inquisitors of the Holy Office—today called the Congregation for the Doctrine of the Faith—can no longer burn heretics at the stake.

Harrie Salman presents a way out of this tragically polarized situation, in which people on both sides tend to believe that those on the other side have been "brainwashed." He coolly and succinctly identifies the pieces of the puzzle and puts them together in a coherent pattern that anyone, of any political persuasion, can recognize.

To those readers who dismiss the advancement of the ideas Harrie puts forward in this book with justifiable skepticism, I have a simple, respectful request.

Please momentarily suspend your disbelief, follow the arguments Harrie makes and then, if you wish, take the time to go to his extensive notes and check out the documentation he provides for yourself.

If you choose to do so, you will be richly rewarded.

Foreword to the American Edition

Living in an Artificial World

In Corona times we live in a world with new dividing lines running across families, circles of friends and other social groupings. The polarizing question revolves around where we stand on our government's Corona policy, in whatever nation we may live. In the United States that question has become highly politicized, which makes it difficult to form and express an independent opinion without being pushed into one of the political corners. The Corona debate has given rise to several related questions: On which level should health policy be made? Which interest groups are involved? Does current health policy have a scientific basis? The ultimate question, however, is this: How we can protect our health as individuals and as members of our families and other social groups?

For ease of use, I have created for this book the terms "Corona times," "Corona society," "Corona crises" and similar usages. In doing so, of course, I have taken a liberty with the now globally famous word "coronavirus," for the purpose of highlighting the way the entire world has become obsessed with a microscopic virus to which all kinds of magical and destructive powers have been attributed by leaders in medicine, public health, business, and government. As more than one writer has pointed out, this virus has been described in relation to the word "corona" because, when observed under a microscope, it appears to glow and is surrounded by an aura that has been dubbed a "corona." The term "corona," however, also refers to what dictionary.com describes as "a white or colored circle or set of concentric circles of light seen around a luminous body, especially around the sun or moon." It is also a term that refers to "something suggesting a crown." While our world's authorities have apparently given a crown to this virus, attempting to give it a place in ruling our world, I suggest it is much more helpful to think of the virus' "corona" simply as a form of light, which hopefully might illumine our minds and hearts in liberating ways, free of fear.

Here are the issues and conflicts with which we are confronted, as I see them:

1. Globalism vs. Localism

One of the main developments of the last decades is globalization. American political interests created a global sphere of influence in which international corporations could thrive. Although many members of the world's middle classes have benefited from those corporations, there now exists a general feeling among many people in many nations that the relation between global and local interests is out of balance, as populist political movements show in Europe and the US. The Corona crisis raised the question of on which level the epidemic should be managed. Should it be managed rightly internationally by the World Health Organization (WHO), federally by the US and other national governments, by the individual states within countries, or by local health authorities? It appears that only on the lower levels of governments is it possible for the management of the Corona crisis to be under democratic control.

2. Big Business vs. Small Business

The Corona crisis benefits, above all, the pharmaceutical companies. It is also highly beneficial for the big tech corporations and their shareholders. In many European countries non-essential shops, restaurants, cafés, and cultural organizations had to close for several months in 2020 and again in the winter of 2020/21. In the early spring of 2021 in some countries these shops were open by appointment to a limited number of customers at the same time. The lockdowns ruined many small businesses and brought new customers to internet businesses and "big box" stores in malls.

3. Materialistic Science vs. Holistic Science

The scientific basis of the Corona policies is severely criticized by many independent physicians and scientists as well as by professional practitioners of holistic therapies such as anthroposophical medicine, homeopathy, traditional Chinese medicine, naturopathic medicine, and other disciplines. Official medicine regards the human body as a biochemical machine. Authorities in the medical establishments around the world do not advocate for practices which enhance the natural immunity of human beings. Nor, for that matter, do they believe that diseases and epidemics contain a message for individuals who became ill, or for humanity at large. Holistic practitioners, in contrast, tend to look at human health as a balance of forces that are continuously disrupted and need, through holistic therapies, to find a healthy balance all the time.

4. Collective Responsibility vs. Individual Responsibility

The essential question is this: Who is responsible for my personal health? Many people have handed over this responsibility to a medical establishment that does not heal them but keeps their chronic diseases under control. Faced with an exorbitantly expensive medical system, a growing number of Americans are taking the challenge to change their lifestyles and their food habits, consult holistic therapists and medical doctors, and take care of themselves for their general health and in Corona matters.

In the general population of most countries different positions are taken. One group is not sure about what to think of the Corona crisis, while others have expressed outspoken opinions, either in favor of the official policies or against them. In this book, I have set myself the task to present my unique analysis of the current situation, based on considerable research, which I will document in the references throughout the book. I hope that the evidence I present and the arguments I bring forward in this book will be useful to readers who may agree with my analysis, and to readers who may disagree with my views on the present situation. Above all, I will describe what I see as the symptoms of a grave illness of our societies, resulting from the way they are organized and from our alienation from nature. It is a societal illness that became visible once again in the Corona epidemic and in the way our governments wage a war against the Coronavirus. It is my aim to offer some new thoughts and suggestions about how we may work together to heal this social illness, and to protect our health as individuals and as members of our families and other groups.

As a philosopher of culture and social scientist from Holland I do not want to take a position on the American political battlefield. It is my intention to contribute to a rational discussion based on facts that anyone can check, and to an understanding of the larger framework of the social transformation we are currently undergoing. The World Economic Forum and its executive director Klaus Schwab promote this transformation as "The Great Reset," in a global campaign for the new technological revolution carried out by the major international corporations. It is my observation that, at present, there is, generally, more awareness and criticism of this project in Europe than elsewhere in the world. I hope this book will raise awareness and stimulate healthy debate about the Great Reset in other countries, as well.

This Great Reset has the support of the promotors of global governance, leaders of big business and materialistic scientists. The social vision expressed by the leaders and supporters of the Great Reset has its roots in the science of social engineering that was developed in the early 1930s at Columbia University and led to the Technocracy movement.[1] Those scientific ideas were first applied in Roosevelt's New Deal and have ever since promised the construction of a more perfect society by science and technology, under the supervision of technocrats, among them social scientists and public relations specialists. The people who are the driving forces behind the Great Reset form a power circle representing the political, economic, and scientific interests of our time. In the past decades they transformed agriculture, public services, healthcare, school education into sectors that generate big profits for the financial elites of our world. Now they celebrate the introduction of new technologies as a multiple trillion-dollar investment market, as the American tech expert and investment advisor Jeff Brown is proclaiming.[2]

Nevertheless, the new technological revolution is meeting with resistance from many people across the world. They are involved in local civil society groups, small private or cooperative businesses, holistic science and in groups focussed on the development of individual, social and ecological consciousness. Their main concern is that the new technological changes will dehumanize us by fundamentally changing our way of life. These changes will separate us further from the natural world and from the immediate relationship with our inner life and our fellow human beings. How we want to live with technology is the decisive question. The Corona crisis introduced new psychological and social techniques (spreading of fear, social distancing, lockdowns) for dealing with the epidemic, and technological

---

[1] Patrick M. Wood, *Technocracy Rising*, 2015, and *Technocracy – The Hard Road to World Order*, 2018 both published by Coherent Publishing, Mesa (AZ).

[2] www.youtube.com/watch?v=sbwS-WvMOD0.

innovations, such as a new kind of vaccine. All such measures, I would argue, are part of the Great Reset.

In a globalized economy we need institutions of global governance, but as practiced now through the health dictatorship global governance is causing the loss of autonomy at lower levels. On a supranational level the rules are determined by powerful interest groups. Individual states no longer have any influence on this movement toward centralized control, and in many respects the democratic voice of the people has also become meaningless. Decisions on matters that are important to everyone are made by technocrats controlled by international lobby groups. Thus, we are being led into a world without cash, a world penetrated by dangerous 5G electromagnetic frequencies, cars without drivers, genetic manipulation, and ubiquitous camera surveillance with facial recognition. The current political debate in many countries—to the extent that it is allowed to take place in public—pits people who want to leave the shaping of the future to international interest groups against people who want to give citizens the decisive democratic voice in developing our society.

This technological and political revolution, what Klaus Schwab and others call "the Fourth Industrial Revolution," is driven by people who advocate a science and a technology that, they suggest, must dominate our world to improve it. They are not held in check by a moral conscience. Science, as presently practiced in the mainstream institutions, only explores the material aspects of reality, while its funding is increasingly determined by economic and military interests. Independent research in which basic questions of the scientific world view are addressed is disappearing for lack of funding. What takes place in science also takes place in other areas of culture. Independent opinion-forming is not promoted in the general population of the world, as public opinion is controlled by a few large media corporations.

This revolution raises some fundamental questions concerning human health. During the Corona epidemic a new health management policy was promulgated worldwide by the WHO for all its member countries. That policy stipulates how sovereign members states of the WHO should deal with epidemics. For that purpose, some definitions related to infectious diseases were changed. As early as 2009, the WHO had revised the definition of a pandemic, so that an infectious disease spreading in several countries in at least two WHO regions would be called a "pandemic." The severity and high lethality of the infectious disease were no longer necessary conditions for the term "pandemic" to be applied.[3] In 2020, a COVID-19 disease case (with an infection caused by the Coronavirus), previously determined by a medical diagnosis, was redefined as a person with a positive PCR test, although that test is not suitable for diagnosis at all. Moreover, since October 12, 2020, the WHO's Director-General, Dr. Tedros Adhanom Ghebreyesus, declared in a media briefing on COVID-19: "Herd immunity is a concept used for vaccination, in which a population can be protected from a certain virus if a threshold of vaccination is reached…. In other words, herd immunity is achieved by protecting people from a virus, not by exposing them to it."[4] In earlier times, herd immunity (the immunity of a population) was defined as the life-long

---

[3] In this book, the common word "epidemic" is used because the word "pandemic" should be reserved for worldwide, very deadly epidemics such as the Spanish flu of 1918/19.

[4] https://www.who.int/director-general/speeches/detail/who-director-general-s-opening-remarks-at-the-media-briefing-on-COVID-19---12-october-2020

immunity that results in a natural way from people having gone through an infectious disease.

When the Corona epidemic began, policies and practices that might have bolstered the natural immunity among the peoples of the world were not even considered by health authorities. The virologists associated with the WHO told us that everyone, even a healthy person, was potentially susceptible to the virus and therefore dangerous to others. The WHO and our governments, acting on their recommendations, told us that everyone should protect themselves, be confined at home in a lockdown (as happened in many countries), and would need a vaccination, indeed a new kind of vaccination that had not even been tested in a proper manner and introduced at the end of its clinical trials. The leadership of the WHO informed the people of the world that we need this vaccination technology so that new viruses can be combated quickly, and hospitals will no longer be overcrowded during epidemics. In so doing, the WHO and others acting as their agents throughout the world, stoked a great fear of the coronavirus. In my opinion, the deliberate creation of an atmosphere of great fear was crucial to their efforts to vaccinate the great majority of the people of the world as a first step toward the introduction of this new technological revolution.

The paradox of the "war" against the coronavirus is that all the restrictive measures imposed in the name of protecting public health damage natural immunity. Nevertheless, even during the lockdowns, many people have maintained a healthy lifestyle and as a result have good natural immunity. They have no fear. The scientific worldview of virology, which sees viruses as a threat and wants to replace life-long natural immunity with temporary artificial immunity through vaccination, is not right for them. Independent researchers share this view. They discovered that experimenting with human immunity has dangerous consequences that are ignored by the pharmaceutical companies.

Instead of the new technological revolution in which all health management will be based upon vaccination, the peoples of the world need and deserve a transformation of our medical systems in the direction of holistic health management policies and practices. With the eventual evolution of a good, holistic healthcare system in our world, in which people learn how to practice healthy lifestyles and promote healthy living conditions, people will develop strong natural immunity. Without the development of such a new, holistic healthcare system, new epidemics and ever new vaccinations programs seem unavoidable.

The Corona crisis may raise the question of how long we want to go on living in an artificial world. Many people live with damaged immune systems, and our inherent human intelligence is in danger of being displaced by artificial intelligence. In our relationships with others, natural contact is disappearing in favor of virtual contact. Our children's play is being replaced by addiction to gaming on handheld electronic devices, and internet lessons have become a substitute for the inspiring teacher-student relationship. In the agricultural word, artificial fertilizer has made our soils infertile, and our genetically modified, glyphosate-saturated food has become artificial and toxic, deprived its full life force.

In our society, too, natural ways of social life are being lost. Our societies are ill because our culture is no longer a natural realm for free spiritual life and democracy has become a façade for a system in which the interests of the people do not play a role. In addition, the economy is a predatory system that exploits people and destroys the earth.

The disappearance of the natural world continues apace. Materialistic science and technology have caused it, economic interests are driving it and politicians representing these interests are allowing it to happen. If we recognize these developments, search for objective facts and are prepared to form our opinion about them, we have the right precondition for an understanding of the crisis caused by the worldwide Corona strategy of the WHO. Reclaiming the natural world is a common challenge that transcends all differences of opinion and political party affiliation. Through reclaiming the natural world and our connection to it, we can awaken to the abnormality of the Corona regime. The current world crisis can become the occasion for the conscious design of a world in which we can once again live humanely with each other and harmoniously with nature.

Harrie Salman, August 2021

Foreword to the Dutch Edition

The Redeeming Christmas Vaccine

At the end of 2020, in many European countries, lockdowns came into effect for the second time. For many weeks we were told by authorities that we were to have as little contact with each other as possible. That restriction, we were told, was to limit the transmission of all viruses so that hospitals would not be overloaded. On December 20, 2020, fearing a new wave of infections, European countries closed air traffic from the United Kingdom for a few days because a mutation of the Coronavirus had been discovered there. This new mutation, it turned out, had been detected already in September 20, 2020.[5] Close to the end of the Brexit negotiations, however, the new mutation became big news, as if a smoke screen were necessary in case they would fail.

Although the scientific research had not been completed, the media immediately assumed that the new mutation was much more contagious than the original Coronavirus. That

---

[5] https://www.cdc.gov/mmwr/volumes/70/wr/mm7003e2.htm

assumption does not seem now to have been accurate. A medical report published on April 22, 2021, noted increased transmissibility but not greater severity.[6] Government advisors feared the worst, as they always do. Curfews were imposed in many European countries. It seems to me no coincidence that the sowing of this new panic coincided with the beginning of the vaccination campaign. All the while, independently of our fears and preoccupations with new strains, the Coronavirus is constantly mutating.[7] On April 1, 2021, the number of identified mutations was already 12,700,[8] some of which become dominant for a time and then disappear.

The main, ostensible goal of the WHO's Corona policy directives is to ensure that all sick people can be cared for in hospitals. Such an assurance requires enough intensive care beds and, above all, enough nursing staff. In many countries both such resources have been permanently cut back in recent years. The Corona crisis, from the point of view of the officials in the WHO and others who set policy, is essentially a crisis in health care capacity. With lockdowns we are paying the bill for a health policy that sees hospitals as businesses. In this business model, there is no more room in hospitals for people suffering from infectious disease epidemics. Vaccines must then, it is reasoned by the authorities, provide a technological solution.

In March 2020, lockdowns were justified by the expectation that the new Coronavirus was a "killer virus" that, without governments taking remedial action, would kill half a million

---

[6] https://www.medicalnewstoday.com/articles/b-1-1-7-variant-increased-transmissibility-but-not-greater-severity

[7] https://www.cdc.gov/coronavirus/2019-ncov/variants/variant.html

[8] https://srhd.org/news/2021/coronavirus-mutations-and-variants-what-does-it-mean

people in the UK and more than one million in Germany. It quickly became clear, however, that the lethality of the virus was not much greater than that of a flu virus and that the immune systems of almost all healthy people under the age of 70 were strong enough to cope with it. I will explain this important point in detail in the body of this book.

The population of every country has been kept under the pressure of fear. In her emotional speech on December 9, 2020, German Chancellor Angela Merkel said that if we have too much contact with others, next Christmas could be the last with the grandparents. Even before that speech, however, children in Germany were urged not to cause the death of their grandparents. Such speech is moral blackmail.

In all countries, the number of deaths attributed to the Coronavirus has been rising since the fall of 2020. The question here, however, is whether that reported increase of deaths is caused only by the Coronavirus or also by flu viruses that always spread in the population in fall. All the new restrictive social measures and the expectation of more deaths increase the fear of the virus and increase the willingness to get vaccinated. Fear of the virus is perhaps the most important factor in the infection. Fear undermines our natural immunity, as is known from psychoneuroimmunology.

The media eagerly awaited the arrival of the so-called vaccines. On December 14, 2020, Dutch Prime Minister Rutte said: "With the vaccine, 2021 will be a year of hope and light at the end of the tunnel." In this way, the Christian expectation of salvation of the Christ Child, who redeemed the world from evil, was projected onto the vaccine, which will redeem the world from the Coronavirus. The vaccines are touted as the salvation of humanity, but we do not know if they will protect against the Coronavirus, or how long they will protect, or if they will be safe in the long run, because all these products were rushed to market before the end of clinical trials under emergency authorizations. We also still do not know if people can still transmit the virus to others after vaccination.

Government policy in the Corona era raises many questions among responsible citizens. There is a great lack of transparency in this policy, which has turned thousands of people into Corona researchers. They do not get answers to their questions in the mainstream media, which only uncritically follows the official policy. Moreover, in social media and on YouTube, critical comments and videos are deleted. Therefore, many questions remain unanswered that require a parliamentary investigation in every country.

Many people have questions about:

- the real danger of the virus;

- the deliberate spread of fear;

- the immunity that exists in the majority of the population;

- the non-infectiousness of people without symptoms;

- social distance for people who have no symptoms;

- the scientific basis of the lockdowns;

- the attribution of all flu-like symptoms to the Coronavirus;

- the models used by the advisory health institutes;

- the non-comparison of the number of so-called Corona deaths with the number of people who die of flu in other years;

- the actual usefulness of masks to cover the mouth;

- the reliability and specificity of the PCR test;

- the labelling of every person who tests positive as a person infected with the Coronavirus;

- the failure to test people for other viruses;

- the policy of closing schools and universities, museums, cafes, restaurants, hotels, and shops that are unlikely to cause infections;

- the ruining of the cultural sector and small business owners;

- the conflict of interest between health agencies and the pharmaceutical industry;

- who really needs a vaccine.

An investigation into non-transparent government information led to my research report *The Corona Epidemic* in June 2020. It was based on expert evidence presented in scientific journals and on the internet, and questioned the assumptions that governments present about the Coronavirus. Those assumptions include the following ideas:

- The SARS-CoV-2 virus is a completely new virus.

- No one is immune to this virus.

- All flu-like symptoms are presently caused by it.

- Someone without symptoms can transmit the virus.

- Anyone who tests positive is infected with the virus.

- Everyone is potentially dangerous to others.

- People can infect each other outdoors.

- Face masks offer protection against viruses.

- There is no early treatment of the illness.

- Only a vaccine can end the epidemic.

Each of these assumptions is highly questionable. According to independent experts and researchers they are not true.[9] Nevertheless, government policies of lockdown, social distancing and face masks rely on them, even though they have no solid scientific basis. This policy is set in an international context in which agreements have been reached, under the leadership of the WHO, on the measures to be implemented in the event of a certain number of cases of the disease or positive tests. Those measures are then made acceptable through a targeted media strategy of fear. Similarly, high-level agreements have been reached on a new generation of vaccines to be introduced after an unprecedentedly short testing period. This international context is the Great Reset. While the world has been terrified, international business has hit the reset button. It is abolishing democracy and setting up the world for an international technocratic dictatorship with the help of modern technologies whose

---

[9] Scientific evidence will be referred to in Chapter 1.

application promises great profits. It is time for the people to take back the power and wealth that big business has usurped. We need to shape the world together in the interests of all humanity.

Harrie Salman, The Netherlands, January 28, 2021

Introduction

A Unique Window of Opportunity

According to Klaus Schwab (b. 1938), founder of the World Economic Forum, the Corona epidemic offers a "unique window of opportunity" for social change. At this annual forum, leaders of the international business community meet to discuss the state of the world and coordinate strategies to achieve their goals. They represent the interests of the world's rich who have invested their wealth in big business. The political leaders of numerous countries are their guests, as are representatives of the international media, who shape public opinion.

The Forum announced in May 2020 that the next annual meeting would focus on *The Great Reset*, the reboot of the global economy. Due to the epidemic, the Forum was postponed from January to May 2021. Executives from major companies would then discuss with invited politicians, intellectuals, and journalists how the epidemic would offer opportunities to "collectively and urgently lay the foundations for a global economic and social system for a more equitable, sustainable and resilient future," as the announcement said.

In December 2020, the postponed meeting was called off. Instead, a Special Annual Meeting will be held in Singapore from August 17 to 20, 2021, where world leaders from economics, politics and civil society will discuss the global recovery from the Corona epidemic. The Forum meeting, originally scheduled for January 25-29, 2021, became a digital conference dedicated to the theme of *Harnessing Technology for Environmental Sustainability*. The goals of the Great Reset continue to set the agenda for the work of the World Economic Forum. The Great Reset is about:

- Justice (focus on the common good);

- Sustainability (the climate change agenda);

- Innovation (clearing the way for new technologies).

In the run-up to this meeting, Klaus Schwab and Thierry Malleret wrote the book *COVID-19: The Great Reset*, which was published in 2020.[10] It offers an insight into the ideas that live within the minds of the world's elites. Here, we should distinguish between the richest 1% of the world who own 50% of the world's wealth (the financial elite), the top of international business (the economic elite) and the leading international politicians (the political elite). Remarkably, Schwab and Malleret represent a vision that is not in line with mainstream neoliberal views, a vision that recognizes the problems created by globalization. Schwab is a strong proponent of the Fourth Industrial

---

[10] Klaus Schwab and Thierry Malleret, *COVID-19: The Great Reset*, Forum Publishing, Geneva 2020.

Revolution, which began at the beginning of the 21st century and has now accelerated.

In Schwab and Malleret's book the authors describe the world's major problems from the perspective of the global elites. Are the goals of the protection of human dignity, the development of a just society and the care of nature really in good hands with them? That, in my opinion is the big question.

The plans of the elites, which in my opinion are not in the best interest of humanity, force us to take responsibility for ourselves and to take actions based on our own visions. As I described in my 2019 book *Gestolen welvaart* (*From Private Wealth to Shared Well-Being*), a different reset is needed. As part of a fundamental societal transformation, stolen wealth can become shared prosperity, and responsible stewardship of nature can become possible.

This present book on the Great Reset looks at the future of our society. It also concludes with some suggestions for how we can live healthy, responsible, self-directed lives in touch with Nature and with the world of Spirit, in the face of the social and technological changes we are currently witnessing.

In the first chapter, I describe the kind of society in which we are living in what I call "the Corona era." In the second chapter, I then detail the Great Reset, the global elite's plan to create a global technocratic dictatorship and explain how the expected Corona epidemic provides an opportunity to carry out this plan. In the third chapter, I analyze the rise of the biosecurity state. In the fourth chapter, I explore how the Corona epidemic may lead to a world order in which the big corporations take control. In the fifth chapter, I consider how the emergence of this world order raises the question of what kind of worldview is being propagated under the banner of the Great Reset. In the sixth chapter, I lead up to a reflection on the future of our society. In the concluding seventh chapter, I reflect that while society is out of balance, and so are our personal lives, everyone can do something about it. I also provide some specific examples of ways in which we can take action to do something positive.

The Corona Society

The Constitution of the United States of America, which went into effect on March 4, 1789, and is the oldest written constitution in the world, begins with the following three, simple but powerful words: "We the people." Those words introduce a document that, in its entirety, affirms that the government of the United States exists to serve its citizens. It is a "government of the people, by the people and for the people," as Abraham Lincoln said in 1863.

Let us leave aside for the moment the question of whether we can, in fact, exercise the powers inherent in the words "We the people" by voting once every couple of years. There is no question, however, that since the introduction of the measures to combat the Coronavirus in March 2020 the relationship between the people and the ruling circles has come under stress not only in the United States of America but throughout the world. Legislative bodies around the world have largely given up their legislative and independent policy-making functions and almost without exception agreed in advance to all measures to be taken as recommended by the World Health Organization. In that manner, health dictatorships were established in many countries of the world. This transnational health dictatorship came into power via temporary legislation under declarations of a health emergency.

In the United States, President Trump had his own White House Coronavirus Taskforce, replaced by the COVID-19 Response Team by President Biden. Trump and Biden had contrasting approaches to the Corona crisis. Trump, for example, endorsed the use of hydroxychloroquine but also supported Operation Warp Speed, the military and intelligence dominated effort to get the vaccines produced at record speed. Trump also suggested that the virus came from China, and vulgarly called it the "Kung Fu Virus," before it became politically unacceptable to associate the virus with China. Trump's administration also gave funding to Children's Health Defense and other organizations critical of the COVID-related "vaccines," and was criticized for doing so in the mainstream press. Biden has had nothing to say about cheap alternative treatments and has been a cheerleader for vaccines. In May 2021 he has stated he wants an official investigation into the origins of the virus, opening the door to the possibility it may be officially recognized as having come from the lab in Wuhan.

Typical of the American situation is that governors of the states have their own responsibility, which led to significant differences in the Corona policies. We may look at the examples of California and Florida, where different approaches led to rather comparable outcomes in terms of cumulative COVID-19 deaths per 100,000 inhabitants from March 2020. Until June 6, 2021, California had 160.2 deaths per 100,000, and Florida had

179.5 per 100,000.[11] The analysis of the differences between the states is of course a matter of serious dispute. Researchers from the University of Chicago's Harris School of Public Policy, in a paper published on April 21, 2021, found that during the virus' first U.S. surge last spring, shelter-in-place orders had no detectable health benefits, only modest effects on behavior, and small but adverse effects on the economy.[12]

The US government is advised on Corona by virologists from the National Institute of Allergy and Infectious Diseases (NIAID) led by Anthony Fauci, MD. It cooperates with other institutes whose work is coordinated by the WHO, the World Health Organization. This organization is co-financed by the Bill & Melinda Gates Foundation, the largest private foundation in the world.[13] This foundation has assets of about $50 billion, of which about $36 billion was donated by Bill Gates. The interests of the pharmaceutical industry are served by leading figures in the American health sector who have connections of a financial nature with this industry. The pharmaceutical industry exerts its influence not only through lobbyists, but mainly through its representatives who hold important positions in the health technocracy, such as Fauci.

One of the main financial interests, and indeed one of the top profit-centers of this industry is the sale of vaccines. In 2009, the WHO declared swine flu a pandemic and governments bought billions of euros worth of vaccines, but they were

---

[11] https://www.latimes.com/projects/california-coronavirus-cases-tracking-outbreak/

[12] Christopher R. Berry, a.o., Evaluating the effects of shelter-in-place policies during the COVID-19 pandemic, at https://doi.org/10.1073/pnas.2019706118

[13] The Gates Foundation is the second largest sponsor of the WHO after the United States. See: www.weforum.org/agenda/2020/04/who-funds-world-health-organization-un-coronavirus-pandemic-COVID-trump/

hardly used because there were very few deaths worldwide.[14] The Corona epidemic was also initially presented as extremely dangerous in 2020. As we will make clear, it soon turned out that this was not the case. Klaus Schwab of the World Economic Forum conceded already in July 2020 that "COVID-19 doesn't pose a new existential threat."[15] Nevertheless, according to the German prime minister Angela Merkel, "the pandemic will not disappear until we really have a vaccine," as she said publicly on April 9, 2020.[16] Governments have spread fear to ensure that people complied with the measures taken and held out the prospect of a vaccine as a salvation. Investors in the pharmaceutical industry could be particularly happy with the purchase of Corona vaccines, in principle for everyone in the world. "This vaccine we're gonna give to 7 billion people," Gates said to the German public in an interview in the evening news on Easter Sunday, April 12, 2020.

Documents from the German Ministry of Health (the so-called "Panic Paper"), which speak about a "desired shock effect," and from SAGE, the UK government's advisory group, show that officials spread fear deliberately.[17] What price does society pay for spreading fear? People became afraid of each other and saw the other as a source of danger. Governments forced people to keep their distance and used that restriction to ban demonstrations as well! The shaking of hands in greeting

---

[14] See the documentary *Profiteers of Fear*, 2009, www.youtube.com/watch?v=lR3pXGQ_tqI.

[15] Schwab and Malleret, *COVID-19: The Great Reset*, p. 15.

[16] https://www.welt.de/politik/deutschland/article207167375/Merkel-zu-Corona-Solange-wir-keinen-Impfstoff-haben-wird-das-gelten.html

[17] www.abgeordnetenwatch.de/sites/default/files/media/documents/2020-04/bmi-Corona-strategiepapier.pdf and Mike Yeadon, Science, SAGE, Ferguson, Immunity, 2020, www.youtube.com/watch?v=ZrPTTgAFZnE. On the role of the UK government see: Laura Dodsworth, A State of Fear, Pinter & Martin Ltd, London 2021.

others was frowned upon. In countries such as Italy and France, for several months people were locked up in their homes, and they were only allowed to leave to buy food within a limited radius. In countries with lighter forms of lockdown, people were only allowed to socialize with a few other persons. Wearing face masks was made compulsory on public transport and in shops. Those who did not comply were in many countries punished with heavy fines. In many countries, police have used excessive force against peaceful demonstrators. As a result of the measures, society lost its internal cohesion, and many people became socially isolated.

In the second round of lockdowns, people without symptoms (i.e., who cannot infect others) are again asked to avoid contact with others. Schools, museums, cafés, restaurants, and shops for non-essentials are closed again. Only one or two guests could be received at home, and in Great Britain having a visitor was even forbidden for several months until early April 2021. A curfew came into force across France as early as December 15, 2020. Other countries followed with their own curfews later after a new, supposedly more contagious virus mutation emerged in Great Britain, and others in South Africa and Brazil.

Corona society has several characteristics of a totalitarian society. The wearing of face masks is seen by many as a symbol of submission to a totalitarian regime. We know such regimes from history. They eliminate democracy by introducing a state of emergency and keep people under control by spreading fear and imposing absurd punishments on those who do not play by the rules. They break resistance by force. They control the media and allow half-truths and outright lies to be spread. Scientific knowledge is used selectively and thus becomes an instrument of power. A totalitarian society develops with an 'iron logic' of rationally justified measures, as the philosopher Hannah Arendt noted.[18] Supporters of the totalitarian ideology, in this case the protection of public health, treat those who do not accept the biosecurity measures with hostility. Society is atomised into a mass of single individuals who can be controlled because there is a danger, an enemy that must be eliminated. In this case, it is a virus that is expected to cause the breakdown of the health-care system.

In this society, health technocrats enforce a disciplining of our behavior by imposing hygiene rules on us that run counter to normal human behavior; constantly disinfecting our hands, keeping our distance, no longer hugging and kissing dear human beings, no longer singing, eating, and celebrating together, going to the pub or church. The German philosopher Matthias Burchardt called this the emergence of *homo hygienicus*, the human being who must be protected from viruses and bacteria by imposing rules of conduct. In this way, the natural immunity that humans have built up over thousands of years in dealing with viruses can no longer develop properly.[19] We lose sight of the causes of epidemic diseases. They are the result of poverty, polluted water, our intrusion into the animal world, global travel and weakened immunity. The appearance of dangerous viruses can also be understood as a spiritual message that our lives have lost their natural harmony.

---

[18] Hannah Arendt, *The Origins of Totalitarianism*, 1951.

[19] Matthias Burchardt im Gespräch, November 25, 2020, www.youtube.com/watch?v=h-y2h-St9uOY.

Government policy is not about improving health care because the number of deaths attributed to Corona is dwarfed by the number of victims caused by the arms industry, the tobacco industry, air pollution and the stressed pace of modern life. Most of the people who died from COVID-19 were old (the average age being over 80) and suffered from diseases of affluence (heart disease, diabetes, obesity). Instead of improving people's health, a biotechnological solution is chosen. With a new kind of vaccine, the pharmaceutical industry wants to artificially stimulate the human immune system, which develops naturally by passing through diseases. This is being done in a worldwide medical experiment. With such vaccines, epidemics can be fought more quickly in the future. This is one of the aims of the Corona health dictatorship, of which we have learned the following aspects during 2020/21:

This health dictatorship works with false models. Shortly before the lockdowns were announced, English epidemiologist Neil Ferguson (of Imperial College of London) came out with his infamous worst-case scenario on March 16, 2020. According to him, if nothing were done, 60% of the UK population could be infected and in more than 3% of cases this would lead to death. There would then be 510,000 deaths in the UK. That overblown prediction caused panic in the population. For the United States Ferguson similarly predicted 2.2 million Corona deaths.[20] Those scenarios were not based on facts, but on elaborate, pseudoscientific conjecture. Ferguson's predictive work relied on unreliable figures from China. In addition, he posited, without proof, that no human being was immune to the "novel coronavirus"

---

[20] https://www.nature.com/articles/d41586-020-01003-6.

and that, moreover, people without symptoms could still transmit viruses.

In contrast to Ferguson's hyperbolic statements, on March 17, 2020, the renowned Stanford University professor John Ioannidis presented much lower estimates that were based on real research and later proved to be correct. Ioannidis spoke of "a once-in-a-century evidence fiasco" to justify the lockdown policy of governments.[21] He reported on his studies of the outbreak of COVID-19 on the Diamond Princess cruise ship. Among the 700 infected elderly passengers and crew members, 7 persons died (with a few more dying later). For the whole US population, he estimated a case fatality rate (number of deaths compared to diagnosed cases) between 0.05 and 1%. In a recent publication of March 14, 2021, based on much more data Ioannidis estimated that the average global infection fatality rate (number of deaths compared to diagnosed and estimated asymptomatic/non-diagnosed cases) is about 0.15%, which is much less than what Ferguson predicted a year earlier.[22] Corona, Ioannidis demonstrates, was most definitely not the expected "killer virus." Many other scientists are now joining with him in presenting their own research substantiating that assertion.

This health dictatorship ignores scientific research. The Ferguson example makes it clear that the technocrats in charge ignore reliable scientific evidence when it does not suit them. Much research has already been done over the years, so we know that flu viruses (and Coronaviruses) are seasonal and disappear in the

---

[21] John P.A. Ioannidis, A Fiasco in the Making?, www.statnews.com/2020/03/17.

[22] https://onlinelibrary.wiley.com/doi/pdf/10.1111/eci.13554.

summer. Recent studies show that the spread of the Coronavirus in European countries receded autonomously before any interventions became effective, and that lockdowns had no evident impact on the Corona epidemic in 2020.[23] WHO technical lead for the Coronavirus Maria Van Kerkhove reported on June 8, 2020 that asymptomatic transmission seems to be very rare.[24] In December 2020 a city-wide prevalence study of almost 10 million people in Wuhan found no evidence of asymptomatic transmission.[25] On July 23, 2020 epidemiologist Tom Jefferson and professor Carl Heneghan of the Centre for Evidence-Based Medicine in Oxford concluded that there is no evidence that Coronavirus masks make any difference.[26] A scientific review on transmission of the virus concludes that existing evidence supports the wide-held belief this risk is lower outdoors but that there are significant gaps in our understanding of the transmission.[27] Social distancing in the open air therefore makes limited sense. The common-sense rule would be for people with symptoms of COVID-19 to stay inside and to keep distance from others. Good ventilation is required indoors, and children are not at risk. In many countries, however, primary school children have had to wear masks at school. Since March 2020, there has been a wealth of reliable scientific evidence to support such positions from research and

[23] www.aier.org/article/lockdowns-do-not-control-the-coronavirus-the-evidence/ (December 19, 2020)

[24] Peter Sullivan, WHO official: Asymptomatic spread of coronavirus 'very rare', *The Hill*, June 8, 2020.

[25] Allyson M. Pollock and James Lancaster, Asymptomatic transmission of COVID-19, published December 21, 2020, *BMJ 2020;371:m4851*.

[26] Jefferson and Heneghan, www.cebm.net/COVID-19/masking-lack-of-evidence-with-politics/ See the video interview with them at www.youtube.com/watch?v=cK-oAJDXYHg. See also the review Masks Don't Work by the Canadian scientist D.G. Rancourt, June 11, 2020, River Cities' Reader.

[27] T.C. Bulfone and others, Outdoor Transmission of SARS-CoV-2, February 15, 2021, https://academic.oup.com/jid/article/223/4/550/6009483.

from hospital care practice, but it has hardly been considered seriously by persons in positions of authority.

This health dictatorship covers up inadequate health care. The lockdowns were considered necessary because hospital care seemed to be at risk. The media reported extensively on the overcrowded hospitals in northern Italy without mentioning that this happens in every flu epidemic and that only the hospitals of two cities were affected. These are examples of manipulation. Health care in the United States and European countries has been cut back by budget cuts and privatisation; there is no overcapacity, on the contrary, there are too few intensive care units (ICUs), there are too few staff, and the work is poorly paid. Moreover, nursing and care homes have not been able to provide enough protection, so that almost half of the deaths originated there. We are now paying the bill for years of neoliberal cuts in health care. Where people have access to a good healthcare system, can practice healthy lifestyles and enjoy good living conditions the Coronavirus would not cause so many problems. Where a good health care system, healthy lifestyles and healthy living conditions are lacking, we see heavy outbreaks of the epidemic, as in the neighborhoods of impoverished people in many countries, notably Brazil and India.

This health dictatorship ignores natural immunity. When new viruses enter our bodies, our immune system has several lines of defence. Typically, during a flu epidemic, about 5-10% of the population gets sick, mostly without serious symptoms. It was said about the Coronavirus that anyone can get sick. However, there is cross-immunity due to having been infected with other

Coronaviruses that have been present in every flu season for decades.[28] Research done by an American research group showed that more than half of the population is not susceptible to the new Coronavirus and has a T cell-mediated immunity.[29] This can be explained from an earlier exposure to other Coronaviruses. After having analyzed blood samples of healthy donors, a German research group concluded that in 81% of the cases the samples showed T-cell cross-reactivity.[30] Healthy people under 70 can survive a Corona infection without too much trouble (5 out of 10,000 people may die from it), according to the German microbiologist professor Sucharit Bhakdi.[31] The technocrats in charge also seemed unaware or unconcerned that fear and lockdowns weaken immunity. Moreover, the WHO and the world's governments did not make information freely available to the public on natural ways of strengthening immunity.

This health dictatorship exaggerates the danger of the virus. For months, from mid-March 2020, we were bombarded by the media in every news bulletin and on every front page of the newspapers with the latest figures of deaths, hospital admissions and ICU admissions. This created great fear in the population, which made the introduction of the lockdowns acceptable. However, within a few weeks it was clear that the virus was not much more dangerous or deadly than the other four Coronaviruses and the normal flu viruses. It turned out that the 2020

---

[28] A. Yaqinuddin, Cross-Immunity between respiratory coronaviruses, June 30, 2020, https://pubmed.ncbi.nlm.nih.gov/32758887/

[29] Published in *Cell* on June 25, 2020.

[30] Published in *Nature Immunology*, September 30, 2020

[31] https://brightexplorer.com/dr-sucharit-bhakdi-on-coronavirus/. Based on Ioannidis J. The infection fatality rate of COVID-19 inferred from seroprevalence data. Bull World Health Organ 2020.

death rate was in many countries comparable to that of the heavy 2017/18 flu epidemic. Initially it was thought that 3.4% of those who became ill would die, but the infection fatality rate (IFR) is below 0.2%, as Ioannidis concluded, pointing out that in a normal flu season it is about 0.1-0.2% in the United States. That revised infection fatality rate of 0.2% was later confirmed by the WHO. Of course, that number is different for specific age groups and countries, and it varies in time.[32] For healthy people under 70 the IFR is 0.05%.

The Coronavirus can cause complications such as thrombosis and pulmonary lung embolism and long recovery times in about 10% of the cases, probably more than with the different kinds of flu. Despite such features of the Coronavirus, the mainstream media have not done reporting in which they make objective comparisons of hospital admissions, numbers of patients in intensive care units and complications related to the Coronavirus with the same statistics from previous years' flu seasons. The occurrence of infection depends in part on the amount of virus ingested as well as the duration of contact.

While the lockdowns prevented the breakdown of the healthcare system, they could have been lifted after only a few weeks, around Easter, 2020. The technocrats in charge refused to admit their miscalculation, showing that there were, in my opinion, other motives for the lockdowns. Promising early treatments, such as with Hydroxychloroquine, for example, were not applied or forbidden. The fear was to be promoted until a vaccine became available. However, more than 60% of the population

---

[32] Mortality Risk of COVID-19, last update April 22, 2021, https://ourworldindata.org/mortality-risk-COVID.

was probably already immune in Great Britain by the fall of 2020, according to a video in which Mike Yeadon, former Vice-President and Chief Scientist for Allergy and Respiratory Diseases of the leading pharmaceutical company Pfizer, explained the basic immunological aspects of the Coronavirus on November 20, 2020.[33] Compared to heart diseases (20%) and cancer (18%) the Corona infection contributed to about 10% of the death causes, with 343,323 confirmed or presumed COVID-19 deaths, in 2020 in the USA.[34] As I point out below, however, the manner in which deaths were calculated in the USA and other countries is highly questionable.

This health dictatorship counts each deceased person as a Corona death. An important aspect of raising fear was to drive the death toll attributed to the Coronavirus as high as possible. No distinction was made between people who had died from infection with the new Coronavirus (this could be as low as 10-15%) and people who had died from other causes but in whom genetic material from a Coronavirus was found using a PCR test (see below). Other viruses were not tested, although there are five Coronaviruses and the many flu viruses that cause similar symptoms. Everyone who was found to have a virus became a Corona victim. The American medical doctor and psychiatrist Andrew Kaufman raised serious questions about this phenomenon in the reporting of the disease and its associated deaths.[35] He points out that it appears that this practice of declaring all deaths with a positive PCR test as resulting from COVID-

---

[33] See Mike Yeadon, What SAGE has got wrong, 2020, https://lockdownsceptics.org/what-sage-got-wrong/ and his video at: www.bitchute.com/video/J0JWur5LNePt/

[34] https://jamanetwork.com/journals/jama/fullarticle/2778234

[35] Interview on *Unmasking the Lies around COVID-19* at https://andrewkaufmanmd.com/

19 to have be a deliberate policy that received the support of the hospitals because the companies that own the hospitals received substantial US federal funds for reporting each death related to the Coronavirus.

The German health agency went so far as to attempt to prevent the Hamburg professor Klaus Püschel from investigating the exact causes of people's deaths. He did so anyway and found that almost all of them (around 85%) had one or more underlying diseases or were overweight.[36] Most of the so-called Corona deaths died of complications. That happens with all flu deaths and has multiple causes. We also know that many people died from improper treatments, including the administration of oxygen under high pressure. In the early months of the epidemic being placed on a ventilator in New York City hospitals meant a death sentence in 88% of the cases.[37]

This health dictatorship misapplies the PCR test. The Polymerase Chain Reaction (PCR) analysis is a laboratory technique used to find small amounts of DNA in a sample, such as in urine. Prior to its use in the Corona crisis, it was used to detect multiple sexually transmitted diseases, and is still used for that purpose.[38] Invented by Nobel Prize Laureate Kary B. Mullis in 1983, it has also been used to determine which virus made a patient sick after a medical diagnosis. It detects genetic material of a virus but cannot determine whether it is an active virus that has made

---

[36] K. Püschel and J.P. Sperhake, Corona deaths in Hamburg, Germany, June 4, 2020, https://www.ncbi.nlm.nih.gov/pmc/articles/PMC7271134/

[37] Most COVID-19 Patients Placed on Ventilators Died, New York Study Shows. Study conducted from March 1 to April 4, 2020. See www.usnews.com, April 22, 2020.

[38] Polymerase Chain Reaction (PCR) and STD Testing (verywellhealth.com)

someone sick and infectious. It can only detect a suspicion of infection. Nevertheless, this test is used to establish the number of infected people, which is not possible at all. Furthermore, it is not clear how specific the test is, i.e., whether only material from the SARS-CoV-2 Coronavirus is found or also from other viruses. By testing for only one gene sequence (primer) instead of at least three, and by amplifying the material too often (measured by the Cycle threshold or Ct value), the number of positive tests has exploded, which was apparently intended after the summer, as Mike Yeadon argued.[39] How many of such people really carry an active Coronavirus, we do not know. Possibly very few people carry the virus because this test, recommended by the WHO worldwide, is not carried out in laboratories according to a standard procedure. The so-called second Corona wave in the fall of 2020 resulted in fewer hospital admissions and deaths than would have been expected based on the PCR wave of positive tests. The global diagnostic use of this PCR test has justified the December lockdowns. However, it only makes sense to have people with symptoms diagnosed and tested by doctors for all relevant respiratory viruses! Only then can we determine how large the proportion of infections with the Coronavirus really is. On July 21, 2021, the American Centers for Disease Control and Prevention (CDC) announced that the Emergency Use Authorization for the PCR-test will be withdrawn at the end of 2021. Instead, they recommend the adoption of a multiplexed method that distinguishes between Corona and influenza viruses.

---

[39] Mike Yeadon on testing methods, https://lockdownsceptics.org/the-pcr-false-positive-pseudo-epidemic/, updated December 25, 2020.

This health dictatorship controls the media. One of the corner-stones of the health dictatorship is the control of information. The media have become the mouthpieces of governments world-wide. Agreements have been made in all countries to this effect. On TV and in the newspapers, people with critical views were therefore excluded. Corona news of the official agencies is in fact state propaganda and is used to shut down thinking. We are dealing here with internationally organised censorship, which is also laid down in agreements between the WHO and the social media companies. Other views can only be partially dissemi-nated via internet channels such as YouTube, where millions of people become aware of them. Critical videos, however, are systematically removed as so-called disinformation if they do not correspond to WHO views. Such practices form part of a more general censorship by the major social media compa-nies (YouTube, Facebook, Instagram, Twitter, etc.) that takes place without democratic control. In cooperation with Western governments and intelligence services the social media owners introduced their own standards of truth to remove content that is not deemed politically correct. Such unilateral actions constitute a violation of the fundamental right of freedom of expression, guaranteed to the people of most countries by their constitu-tions. To control the spread of information about the Corona epidemic, major social media platforms have shut down access to videos about these matters by some of the world's most respected scientists. Between April and June 2020, in the first months of the epidemic, Google deleted 11.4 million YouTube videos, 2.5 million more than in the same period of 2020. According to Google that increase in deletions is related to their efforts to eliminate "false information" on the virus, vaccines, and all related matters.[40]

This health dictatorship eliminates other expertise. Governments are advised by a small group of virologists. No other expertise is deemed necessary, although it would have been obvious to include general practitioners, economists, sociologists, and psychologists. Governments thus created a "tunnel vision" in which only a few aspects of the crisis are considered. Criticism from other experts is ignored. In many cases, they do not dare to come out with it for fear of their jobs, careers, and future research funds. Those who express doubts about the correctness of government policy in the media, in medicine, at universities or in government are usually muzzled. Freedom of expression is virtually non-existent, therefore, in the discussion of health policy by professionals and officials.

This health dictatorship extols the saving vaccine. From the beginning, governments have promised a vaccine that would end the epidemic. Billions have been spent on vaccine development and governments have mandated vaccines for the entire population. According to Bill Gates, everyone in the world should be vaccinated. Vaccines usually take about 10 years to produce (if at all), and all vaccines have side effects for which the manufacturers are not liable. Government propaganda does not address the potential dangers and possibly highly limited effectiveness of vaccines. Instead, the new vaccines were (provisionally) approved in record time under extreme political pressure.

[40] https://norberthaering.de/medienversagen/militaer-geheimdienste-zensur-youbute-imp-fungitung-der-internet-zensur/

In the United States, President Trump wanted vaccines to be ready before the November 2020 elections, which made scientists worry about political influence over the Coronavirus Vaccine Project, as the headline of an article said.[41]

In all these aspects we can see that the truth is being obscured, but also that science and the media are being deprived of their function of criticism. Governments of the world have become so caught up in the measures internationally imposed under the auspices of the WHO that their officials believe they cannot break away from them even in the face of massive public protests. Citizens are forced to go to court, therefore, to compel their governments to change their policies and practices. Thousands of experts and critical citizens in many countries are calling on their governments to immediately stop all measures and protect only those at risk. To convey this message the epidemiologists Sunetra Gutpa (Oxford University), Jay Bhattacharya (Stanford University) and Martin Kulldorff (Harvard University) wrote the Great Barrington Declaration in October 2020. It has been translated into 43 languages and has been co-signed by 44 medical and public health scientists, mentioned by name, and by 850,000+ others.[42] Their main argument is that the number of healthy life years lost through the Corona measures far exceeds the number of life years gained. In March 2021, Bhattacharya declared that the COVID-19 lockdowns will be remembered as the country's "single worst public health mistake" in the last 100 years.[43]

---

[41] Article with this title written by Sharon LaFraniere and others, *New York Times*, August 2, 2020.

[42] https://gbdeclaration.org/

[43] www.newsweek.com/stanford-doctor-calls-lockdowns-biggest-public-health-mistake-weve-ever-made-1574540.

If we had not known about the new Coronavirus in March 2020, we might have considered it a severe flu epidemic, because clinically the symptoms are the same, with serious complications for some people. We would have been spared, however, being led into a global disaster brought on by the leadership of the WHO and its virologists, aided and abetted by politicians who are ignorant of the dynamics of epidemics of respiratory viruses and at the same time committed to their belief in the vaccination project.

In January of 2021 Knut Wittkowski, a former biostatistician and epidemiologist at Rockefeller University, looked back at the course of the epidemic.[44] He observed that by mitigating the epidemic through lockdowns and other measures, the curve of the infections was flattened, but such a policy prolonged the duration of the epidemic. The lockdowns and related measures, he further observed, caused more deaths. They also led to the rise, in the fall of 2020, of a new epidemic due to resistant mutations, with again more deaths. Wittkowski pointed out that this was the first time in history that an epidemic of a respiratory virus was not allowed to take its course and create herd immunity among young and healthy people, which would have extinguished the epidemic in the northern hemisphere already in May/June 2020. According to Wittkowski, after some three weeks, in April of 2020, all measures could have been lifted, as was originally planned. The peak of infections had already been reached before the lockdowns. Without the lockdowns and with sufficient protection of the vulnerable, according to Wittkowski, only 60,000 Americans might have died. Instead, a new Corona epidemic appeared in the fall of 2020 with the result that the

---

[44] Catching up with Knut Wittkowski, at www.youtube.com/watch?v=J4wIsshE4Q4.

total toll of deaths attributed to COVID-19 deaths up to the time frame of June 2021 was reported as 600,000 mortalities. That high death toll, he claimed, was attributable to the lockdowns and the systemic failures to protect vulnerable populations.

The consequences of the lockdown and other measures that came into effect from mid-March 2020 and again in the fall of 2020 were dramatic. In most countries, the first lockdowns were introduced only after the number of infections had already peaked. Only Sweden did not get involved and respected the freedom of its citizens, as its constitution demands. Sweden's leading epidemiologists chose the path to natural herd immunity. In hindsight, it turns out that regardless of the degree of lockdown, COVID-19 has a similar course everywhere. This was not much different in Sweden than in Italy or the United Kingdom, although Norway and Finland had a much lower death toll, due to the closing of their borders and other factors.[45] We now know that lockdowns have only a marginal impact on the course of an epidemic, unless they are introduced early and maintained over an exceptionally long period of time. For greater impacts to happen, we were told by the authorities, international travel must be restricted. Comparative research carried out in 79 territories and published on November 16, 2020, however, showed that less disruptive and costly non-pharmaceutical interventions can be as effective as more intrusive, drastic, ones, such as a severe national lockdown.[46]

---

[45] Discussed by Johan Giesecke, former Swedish state epidemiologist, in April 2021, at https://www.youtube.com/watch?v=0017zNe7obo.

[46] Nils Haug and others, Ranking the effectiveness of worldwide COVID-19 government interventions, in: *Nature Human Behaviour* 4, p. 1303–1312 (2020).

A lockdown is a social experiment that does more harm than good. Healthy people are locked in, and vulnerable people are not adequately protected because of a failing health system. The consequences of lockdowns can be summarised in a few aspects:

Psychological: confrontation with one's own fear, which can lead to depression and paralyzes the ability to think; educational and psychological problems in children; loss of motivation in children and pupils due to learning via the internet; long lasting trauma in small children due to wearing masks and in adults due to lockdown; sick people who are required to die alone; fear that the other person is a danger to me. In short: loss of humanity.

Social: conflicts and domestic violence due to lockdowns and forced work at home; polarisation between supporters and opponents of the measures; abolition of democracy. In short: disruption of society.

Cultural: the closure of theatres, concert halls, museums, etc., leading to loss of income for those working in this field. In short: the destruction of the cultural sector.

Economic: extreme worsening of inequality, increasing poverty, famine, and unemployment worldwide. In the United States 9.6 million workers lost their jobs in the first 3 quarters of 2020, while in the European Union (with 100 million more inhabitants) only 2.6 million workers lost their jobs.[47] Governments have gone into massive debt to support the corporations and to finance ambitious recovery projects. This has left many countries

---

[47] https://www.pewresearch.org/fact-tank/2021/04/15/fewer-jobs-have-been-lost-in-the-eu-than-in-the-u-s-during-the-COVID-19-downturn/

financially very vulnerable. Many small and medium entrepreneurs will not survive the lockdowns. Their businesses will be taken over by internet shops, big chains, and Chinese investors. The rise in the value of the shares of the companies benefiting from the crisis increased the collective wealth of the 719 American billionaires from $2.95 trillion on March 18, 2020, to $4.56 trillion on April 12, 2021.[48] In summary: for many, the biggest economic crisis since the 1930s.

Medical: sick people are not helped in due time, immunity is weakened by an epidemic of fear, children are exposed to fewer bacteria and viruses (which is necessary for the development of their immune system). In summary, lockdowns are a medical disaster.

The German microbiologist and epidemiologist professor Sucharit Bhakdi has become internationally known for his outspoken criticism of government measures. With his wife, biology professor Karina Reiss, he wrote the book *Corona - False Alarm?*[49] He calls for people to become human again, to take off their masks, to join hands, to embrace, to sing and to ask themselves the question: How and why has our society allowed dehumanisation and the loss of freedom?

---

[48] https://inequality.org/great-divide/updates-billionaire-pandemic/

[49] Karina Reiss and Sucharit Bhakdi, *Corona, False Alarm?*, White River Junction, VT (USA) 2020.

The Great Reset

Changes have been initiated in Corona society that will last. Working from home will be encouraged by companies and shopping from online businesses will increase. Digital education will continue at colleges and universities and, according to the work of Allison MacDowell, expand into elementary and secondary education, threatening to replace traditional school with global workforce development for the Fourth Industrial Revolution.[50] We will see more digital doctor visits, and other professional consultations via computer. Most radically, cash could soon be replaced by digital money and, with the establishment of digital identities on blockchain through the ID2020 project and vaccine passports, governments will be increasingly able to track us with tracing apps.

The business elite see the Corona crisis as a once-in-a-life-time opportunity to reset society. German engineer and economist Klaus Schwab, executive chairman of the World Economic Forum, wanted to hit the reset button for the global economy already back in 2014 because, in his opinion, the world was

---

[50] See her blog site wrenchinthegears.com, and her video library.

still too busy with crisis management instead of fundamental issues. In 2021, the meetings of the Forum are dedicated to the Great Reset.

To better understand this "reset" concept, it is important to also understand some of the other concepts which Schwab and the World Economic Forum are advancing at this time in their effort to create a presumably better world.

In 1971 Schwab developed and began publicizing the concept of "stakeholder capitalism," in which different "stakeholders" cooperate with each other to their mutual benefit. Stakeholder capitalism contrasts with shareholder capitalism, where only the shareholders hold equity in publicly held companies and reap the benefits of company profits. In Schwab's new view, the stakeholders of a company are the capital providers, the employees, the suppliers, the consumers and ultimately society. In this European vision (which includes the "Rhineland model" of consultation with stakeholders), companies have a social responsibility that the large international companies have historically tended to deny, or to which they have given lip service. Due to societal pressure, this is starting to change, so much so that in 2019 the US Business Round Table, a lobby group of 181 executives from large companies, recognized the interests of all stakeholders.[51]

Also in 1971, Schwab founded the European Management Forum to promote the concept of stakeholder capitalism. In 1987 it was rebranded as the World Economic Forum. It functions as a meeting place for top leaders from global business, politics,

---

[51] https://opportunity.businessroundtable.org/ourcommitment/

the media, and representatives of civil society. For Schwab, these are the actors of world society. The Forum sees itself as a global platform for public-private cooperation, defined as cooperation between government and business, and has evolved over 50 years into an organization in which the world's 1,000 largest companies work together to "improve the state of the world." One hundred large companies form the core of the organization as "strategic partners."

Since 1992 the Forum has built a network of 1,300 such leaders. Established as the Global Leaders for Tomorrow, from 2005 onwards the network has been known as Young Global Leaders, whose members are between 30 and 40 years old when elected. Angela Merkel (later German chancellor), Emmanuel Macron (later French president), Jacinda Ardern (later prime minister of New Zealand), Sanna Marin (later Finnish prime minister), Chinese businessman Jac Ma, and Mark Zuckerberg, among others, were elected as members of this network of young leaders.[52] Since 2013, the Forum has built a second network of over 10,000 Global Shapers consisting of people between 20 and 30 years of age. Global Shapers now has over 3,500 alumni. Politicians of both networks can be considered as protégé(e)s of the Davos elites.

The World Economic Forum organizes research in a variety of areas, on which reports are produced that can be downloaded from the Forum's website.[53] The topics of the meetings are discussed in the international press. In addition to the informal deliberations between global leaders, about which nothing is

---

[52] https://www.younggloballeaders.org/community.

[53] www.weforum.org/

disclosed, there are public meetings, videos of which are available. In 2019, for example, we were able to see the young Dutch historian Rutger Bregman call on the world's rich to stop evading taxes and pay their fair share.[54]

In 2020, "Stakeholders for a socially cohesive and sustainable world" was the theme of the Forum's 50th meeting, attended by nearly 3,000 leaders from companies, international organizations, and government agencies. Some young activists who could meaningfully promote the Forum's global goals, such as Greta Thunberg, were also invited. In preparation for this meeting, the *Davos Manifesto 2020* was published in December 2019. It states that the universal goal of business is not only to maximise profits, but also to use knowledge and resources to help solve major world problems in collaboration with governments and civil society organizations. These were the climate crisis and the division of society through inequality and political polarisation. Corporate social responsibility was described in the manifesto in terms of paying fair taxes, fighting corruption, moderate top salaries, and human rights.

The theme of the Great Reset for the post-Corona era, which should have been the focus of the delayed World Economic Forum in January 2021, was prepared by the book *COVID-19: The Great Reset*.[55] It was published in July 2020 by Klaus Schwab and Thierry Malleret, head of the Forum's Global Risk Network programme team. They describe the consequences of the Corona epidemic and argue that it must lead to a reset in economic, social, geopolitical, environmental, and technological policy

[54] Rutger Bregman, www.youtube.com/watch?v=9odkjbkwvWs.

[55] Klaus Schwab and Thierry Malleret, *COVID-19: The Great Reset*, Forum Publishing, Geneva 2020.

areas, as well as for businesses and individuals. They welcome the technological developments accelerated by the lockdown but are also aware of the downsides for people.

The Great Reset is not just about repairing the damage caused by the lockdowns. In their book Schwab and Malleret argue that many problems also needed to be urgently addressed before 2020, and that the Corona epidemic provides an opportunity to do so and make the necessary shifts. The economy must prioritize the well-being of all people and the planet. It must become greener, and the role of the market must be revised. There must be a massive redistribution of wealth from the rich to the poor, from capital to labor. Governments must play a stronger role and taxes will increase to improve social services. In geopolitics, the current lack of global governance must be addressed by a multipolar world order in which the leading nations cooperate with each other. Globalization must become more inclusive, equitable and sustainable, socially and environmentally. On the environmental front, climate change and ecosystem collapse must be addressed. In technology, the authors see an accelerated development, but this can also bring the danger of total control. The economy needs to reorient itself in an environment of rapid automation and technological innovation. The reset for individuals lies in making new moral choices and promoting their well-being.

The delayed January 2021 meeting of the Great Reset Forum aimed to lay new foundations of our economic and social system for a more just, sustainable, and resilient future. This, Schwab said, requires a social contract where human dignity and social justice are at the core. He added: "COVID-19 has accelerated our transition into the era of the Fourth Industrial Revolution. We must ensure that new technologies in the digital, biological and physical worlds remain human-centred and serve all of society providing equal access for all."[56]

Taking note of this vision of the future, one might wonder who would object to the adoption of such seemingly laudable goals. The goals of justice, sustainability and resilience are used to sell the agenda of the new technological revolution and of centralization of control. What is crucial to understand, however, is the context in which this vision is presented. Schwab does not question the economic order of our world. He does not talk about the need for the big corporations and the rich of the world to pay their taxes. Worldwide, countries lose more than $427 billion a year to tax havens.[57]

A fairer future is important, according to Schwab, because growing inequality is increasing unrest in society worldwide. Nowhere is the role of parliaments mentioned, so that it is up to the people of the world to ask about the significance of democracy in the world of the Davos elites. The Davos meetings take place among the leaders of large corporations and political leaders who represent their interests, and not those of their constituencies. The question, therefore, is whether the smaller companies can agree to the various aspects of the proposed resets.

It should also be known that the World Economic Forum has come under sharp criticism from activists opposed to the negative effects of globalization. The issue of the Great Reset is being discussed on websites around the world as a new plan

---

[56] Public announcement of the meeting at the Forum's website.

[57] 2020 *State of Tax Justice* report.

by the evil elites that will lead to growing inequality, threats to property rights, wealth transfers to the rich, higher taxation, a cashless economy, and a totalitarian surveillance state. In the United States, the journalists James Corbett [58] and Del Bigtree, [59] the physician Joseph Mercola and Ronnie Cummins, co-founder and International Director of the Organic Consumers Association, [60] and the entrepreneur Gammon, [61] along with an increasing number of women and men who are thought leaders in many fields have taken public positions that are extremely critical of the Great Reset.

The Fourth Industrial Revolution has been the theme of Forum meetings in 2016 and 2019, and the industrious Schwab has also written books on this: *The Fourth Industrial Revolution* (2016) and *The Future of the Fourth Industrial Revolution* (2018), which testify to his particularly high expectations of technological innovation.[58] The first industrial revolution led to the mechanisation of spinning and weaving by the steam engine in the 2nd half of the 18th century, the second brought the application of electricity and the internal combustion engine a century later, the third (from 1950) was the digital revolution, and the fourth is leading to a multitude of technological developments combining at an accelerated pace since the beginning of the 21st century.

In his 2018 book Schwab describes twelve technologies in which major investments are being made worldwide and which are fundamentally changing our lives. He distinguishes four clusters:

---

[58] Klaus Schwab, *The Fourth Industrial Revolution*, Penguin Random House, 2017. Klaus Schwab, *Shaping the Future of the Fourth Industrial Revolution*, Penguin Random House, 2018.

1. the expansion of digital technologies: new computing technologies; blockchain and distributed ledger technologies for encrypting information; and the Internet of Things (networking of technical devices with each other, e.g., in a smart home or smart city).

2. transformation of the physical world: artificial intelligence, advanced materials and complementary forms of manufacturing and 3D printing.

3. the transformation of the human being: biotechnologies (combining DNA fragments, as in genetic modification); neurotechnologies (such as enhancing and repairing brain functions); and new ways of experiencing reality (virtual and augmented).

4. integration of the environment: capture, storage, and transmission of energy; geoengineering (such as influencing the weather); and space technologies (such as space travel).

The book does not mention digital communications technology (such as 5G) and nanotechnology (working with minutely sized particles) separately, although they too have far-reaching consequences for our lives. 5G wireless networks are being built and put into operation in many countries, while nanoparticles are already used in everyday life, for example in paints, cosmetics, sun protection oil and clothing. The dangers of both technologies are not addressed. Schwab describes the negative consequences that the application of the twelve technologies can have, but his belief in the blessings of technology remains unshakeable.

For Schwab, China is an extremely important partner in the development of the new technology. The World Economic Forum has had good ties with China and Chinese universities for over thirty years. Since 2009, top Chinese politicians, including Xi Jinping in 2017, and leading entrepreneurs have attended Forum meetings.

A critical examination of the role of technology in society is necessary, so let us briefly review some basic features of the evolution of technology. The first three industrial revolutions completely changed our world. They were undoubtedly useful for manufacturers and investors, but for factory workers they brought new forms of slavery and exploitation. The need for raw materials, fuels and markets led to wars and the conquest of almost all territories outside Europe. The fourth industrial revolution now confronts us with the automation of large parts of production and services, which will lead to rising unemployment, not only in the Western world but also beyond. As a palliative measure to planned unemployment, Schwab mentions the possibility of a universal basic income,[59] but such income will come at the price of universal surveillance of individual behavior patterns, creating a continual harvesting of data from millions of human beings, even greater than that which currently occurs via social media usage. In this new technological revolution, data and the processing and sale of data are central. This is also in the interest of governments who want to control their citizens.

The further development of technology, therefore, can become a threat to our humanity, because the development of

---

[59] https://www.weforum.org/agenda/2020/04/COVID-19-universal-basic-income-social-in-equality/

artificial intelligence confronts us with the question of who we are as humans. How is our intelligence different from that of machines? Will our society be taken over by intelligent robots and will we be monitored by cameras with facial recognition software and by sensors under our skin? What are we to make of movements such as transhumanism, which seeks to combine man and machine?[60]

We also need to ask ourselves who wants these new technologies. The people have not opted for 5G, the new networks for mobile communication or for facial recognition techniques, even though taxpayers' money has been used to prepare them. 5G technology was not developed for citizens, but for crowd control by the government, to control the masses with cameras and facial recognition techniques, for the administration of smart cities and the creation of the internet of all things.

---

[60] Nicanor Perlas, *Humanity's Last Stand – The Challenge of Artificial Intelligence*, Temple Lodge, Forest Row (UK) 2018.

The Biosecurity State

Human intrusion into the animal world and industrial farming allows bacteria and viruses from the animal world to be increasingly transmitted to humans. We can think of the bird flu virus and bat viruses. Less well known is that bacteria and viruses also have the attention of the military because of their possible use in biological warfare. This research is officially restricted but continues in major countries with the argument that the population needs to be protected from bioweapons. Bacteria and viruses are therefore studied in laboratories and genetically modified. In this way vaccines can be prepared in advance. Occasionally, a dangerous virus escapes a laboratory. We must ask if the new coronavirus is also a product of bioweapons research and escaped from a lab.

Since early 2020 these questions have indeed been investigated. Research in India and in France by Nobel Prize winner and discoverer of the HIV-virus Luc Montagnier from Spring 2020 led to the conclusion that a part of the virus contained pieces of the HIV-virus.[61] This news was soon repressed. In October 2020 researchers Rossana Segreto and Yuri Deigin argued that the virus could be the result of genetic manipulation.[62] Any suggestion of a lab origin was rejected by the WHO officials and virologists in their service. For political reasons they preferred the Chinese view that the virus had emerged from nature.

In a well-researched article published on January 4, 2021, in *New York Magazine*, journalist Nicholson Baker gathered the evidence for the Wuhan lab origin of the virus, describing the role of all relevant actors involved in the so-called gain-of-function research.[63] This research is carried out to manipulate viruses to make them more dangerous. The American journalist Art Moore analyzed its funding by Anthony Fauci's NIAID. This kind of virus engineering was forbidden by the Obama administration but resumed in 2017 and continued until April 2020 in Wuhan.[64] On May 5, 2021, the leading British science writer Nicholas Wade wrote an article on the origin of COVID that shattered the official opinion.[65] Building upon earlier evidence he showed that the novel Coronavirus was adapted to human cells and therefore had to be made in a lab as a result of gain-of-function research. Such research is part of biowarfare programs across the globe.

Wade's article documented that the research in the Wuhan lab was funded by American taxpayers. The total amount was

[61] Abstract on the Indian research at www.biorxiv.org/content/10.1101/2020.01.30.927871v1. An interview by Montagnier at www.youtube.com/watch?v=GkvRdeUWI6c&t=356s

[62] Segreto and Deigin, 2019, www.youtube.com/watch?v=YcWlRczjDQc.

[63] https://nymag.com/intelligencer/article/coronavirus-lab-escape-theory.html.

[64] www.wnd.com/2021/02/new-evidence-ties-COVID-19-creation-research-funded-fauci/

[65] https://thebulletin.org/2021/05/the-origin-of-COVID-did-people-or-nature-open-pandoras-box-at-wuhan/

nearly $600,000, with EcoHealth Alliance run by Peter Daszak as the intermediary.[66] Between 2014 and 2019 the EcoHealth Alliance received more than $3.7 million in grants from the NIAID to examine the "risk of future coronavirus emergence[s]...in China." Asked by Kentucky Senator Rand Paul on May 11, 2021, at a US Senate Committee, Fauci denied that the NIH and NIAID funded gain-of-function research in Wuhan.[67] He did not deny that the Wuhan lab was receiving funds, but he was obviously using another definition of this research to hide his responsibility.

According to Wade, the first grant in 2014 was formulated in ambiguous terms, and the second grant in 2019 for gain-of-function research was cut off in April 2020 at the order of President Trump, who held the opinion that the virus came from the Wuhan lab.[68] It is known that Fauci, the "global virus tsar" since 1984, does not have an impeccable record, as documented in a report by two investigative journalists published on October 27, 2020.[69]

In his new book, *The Real Anthony Fauci*, to be published in the fall of 2021, Robert F. Kennedy, Jr. exposes how Fauci as the leading public health technocrat dictates the subject, content, and outcome of scientific health research across the globe through the research funds he disburses. Kennedy also exposes how the Pharma-Fauci-Gates alliance exercises dominion over global health policy, which serves to create a new vaccine enterprise

---

[66] https://www.factcheck.org/2021/05/the-wuhan-lab-and-the-gain-of-function-disagreement/

[67] https://www.bitchute.com/video/e98xKdBOwwAa/

[68] https://www.youtube.com/watch?v=2jPYJqFczck

[69] https://off-guardian.org/2020/10/27/anthony-fauci-40-years-of-lies-from-azt-to-remdesivir/

with unlimited growth potential. This alliance proved powerful enough to "wield far-reaching influence and unprecedented power to shut down the global economy, abolish civil and constitutional rights, impose police state surveillance and engineer the greatest upward shift of global wealth in human history."[70]

On May 19, 2021, the report "COVID-19 and the Wuhan Institute of Virology," published by Republican Members of the US House Permanent Select Committee on Intelligence, became a hot news item. It presented the evidence of the NIAIDS' involvement in funding of the gain-of-function research carried out in the Wuhan lab.[71] An article published on June 3, 2021, documented the divide between two groups within the State Department around the investigation of a possible lab-leak origin of the virus. A public discussion of the lab origin would show the involvement of the American government in financing this extremely dangerous gain-of-function research and would also endanger future research in this area.[72]

In early June of 2021 more than 3,200 pages of emails that Fauci wrote during the first half of 2020 were released by media organizations that had obtained them through Freedom of Information Act requests. Besides revealing his day-to-day concerns, the e-mails also confirm his knowledge of the gain-of-function research in the Wuhan lab. That revelation is significant because Senator Rand Paul, in an interview on Fox News in May of 2021, alleged Fauci lied when he testified to Congress that he had no

---

[70] Robert F. Kennedy, Jr., *The Real Anthony Fauci: Bill Gates, Big Pharma, and the Global War on Democracy and Public Health*, Skyhorse Publishing, New York 2021.

[71] https://www.washingtonexaminer.com/news/gop-house-intel-overwhelming-circumstantial-evidence-wuhan-lab-COVID-origin (with download link).

[72] www.vanityfair.com/news/2021/06/the-lab-leak-theory-inside-the-fight-to-uncover-covid-19s-origins.

knowledge of US funding for the gain-of-function research at the Wuhan Institute of Virology.[73] At the time this book went to press it is fair to say that Anthony Fauci was experiencing an unprecedented professional crisis, as chinks in the official story about the Corona crisis have begun to be found through what used to be impregnable walls of obfuscation and secrecy.

The story is, however, much bigger. In the United States, Ralph Baric of the University of North Carolina Chapel Hill, among others, had been researching Coronaviruses since 1999. Much of this research has been funded by the NIAID under the direction of Dr. Anthony Fauci. He funded research by Baric to create an "infectious replication-defective coronavirus" targeted for human lung cells, as the American patent researcher and chairman of M-Cam International Innovation Risk Management, Dr. David E. Martin discovered. This virus appears to be the first SARS (Severe Acute Respiratory Syndrome) coronavirus. On April 19, 2002, Baric and two colleagues sought to patent a method of producing this recombinant coronavirus. This was before the SARS coronavirus outbreak in Asia in 2002/03. In 2007 the U.S. CDC secured a patent for the entire gene sequence of this virus. They also patented the means for detecting it using RT PCR testing. David Martin and his team found more than 4,000 patents relating to SARS coronaviruses. Among them are 120 patents of essential features of SARS-CoV-2 (the so-called "novel" coronavirus from Wuhan) – the polybasic cleavage site,

---

[73] https://www.foxnews.com/media/ran-paul-dr-fauci-lied-congress-china-virus-research

the spike protein and the ACE2 binding.[74] In January 2000 Pfizer patented the first coronavirus vaccine to use the S spike protein. This was a vaccine for canine coronavirus.

When Baric's research was no longer permitted for security reasons, it was outsourced to Shi Zhengli's Institute of Virology in Wuhan in 2014. The National Bio-safety Laboratory of this institute was built in collaboration with the French government's CIRI lab and completed in 2014. Many Wuhan lab staff were trained at a French biosafety lab and there were ties with other labs in the western world. Highly dangerous viruses, among them bat coronaviruses, have been investigated at the Wuhan lab, whose safety status has been questioned by international specialists. Already in 2015 China reduced its cooperation with the French and it ceased completely in 2017. According to David Asher, a former U.S. State Department official, French intelligence officials warned the State Department already in 2015 and again in 2017, expressing grave concerns as to Chinese motivations. According to the State Department, the Wuhan lab has engaged in classified research on behalf of the Chinese military since at least 2017.[75]

The real origin of the coronavirus is not in Wuhan, but in research funded by American health agencies. David Martin discovered that these health agencies and drug companies, who now make the big profits with the vaccines, hold American

---

[74] David E. Martin, The Fauci/COVID-19 Dossier, 2021, https://archive.org/details/the-fauci-covid-19-dossier. Transcript of an interview of David Martin given to the German Corona Investigative Committee on July 9, 2021, https://drive.google.com/file/d/19o1BeQa6z9X-D58GkYE1e-qiiNbnr5wTz/view. See also the review by Dr. Joseph Mercola at https://articles.mercola.com/sites/articles/archive/2021/07/24/patents-prove-sars-cov-2-is-a-manufactured-virus.aspx. A first report of David Martin on the origin of the coronavirus had already been made public on August 18, 2020, at www.bitchute.com/video/kZvYn2cwKJQX/

[75] The Daily Caller News Foundation, July 26, 2021.

patents on the essential features of SARS-CoV-2. To harvest these profits, warnings had to be issued. According to David Martin, the above-mentioned Peter Daszak stated in 2015: "We need to increase public understanding of the need for medical countermeasures such as a pan-coronavirus vaccine. A key driver is the media, and the economics will follow the hype. We need to use that hype to our advantage, to get to the real issues. Investors will respond if they see profit at the end of the process." David Martin concluded: "This was an intentional bio-weaponization of spike proteins to inject into people, to get them addicted to a pan-corona vaccine."[76]

From prevention to preparedness

Virus research as well as measures against the spread of viruses are an essential part of the emerging "biosecurity state." During the Cold War military labs in the leading countries developed biological weapons. After the Cold War in 1989 new health dangers were expected from bioweapons used by terrorists and criminals. In a new step at that time, moreover, epidemics were considered as global health threats. In 2004 the focus of biosecurity shifted in the United States from prevention to preparedness, which involves exercises, simulations, scenario planning and the creation of worst-case scenarios.[77] In the continuous extension of health protection and management we see the rise of the biosecurity state with its proliferation of health security agencies.

---

[76] https://drive.google.com/file/d/19o1BeQa6z9XD58GkYE1e-qiiNbnr5wTz/view, p. 7-8.

[77] Patrick Zylberman, Future as a Moving Target US, in: Serge Morand and Muriel Figuié (ed.), *Emergence of Infectious Diseases*, Editions Quae, Versailles 2018 (Creative Commons)

To secure the state against bioweapons, research is conducted in collaboration with biotechnology institutes. In 1998, the Johns Hopkins Center for Civilian BioDefense Strategies was founded in Baltimore. That institution was later renamed the Center for Biosecurity and is now called the Center for Health Security. Its mission is "to protect people's health from epidemics and disasters and to ensure that communities are resilient to major challenges." That mission gave the Center license to expand research from bioweapons to epidemics spread by terrorists or of natural origin.

Over the past 30 years, the WHO has increasingly grown into the role of a global health ministry. The WHO's experts kept pointing out that a major epidemic could occur unexpectedly, with potentially catastrophic consequences, such as the Spanish Flu epidemic of 1918-19. The WHO's staff and consultants prepared for this possibility over the past three decades by developing pandemic strategies together with national health authorities. The pharmaceutical industry likewise worked to develop new techniques to make vaccines available more quickly. We know that the WHO's main sponsor became vaccine activist Bill Gates, who took an organizing role, in addition to providing massive funding, secondly only to that of the United States. When President Donald Trump cut off US funding of the WHO, Gates became its top donor. President Joe Biden, as expected, restored US funding for the WHO in January of 2021, very shortly after his inauguration.

The Center for Health Security organized several exercises to prepare governments for global health risks. In June 2001, the first exercise, *Dark Winter*, presented a scenario in which a terrorist linked to Bin Laden caused a smallpox outbreak in the United States.[78] Incidentally, that exercise took place shortly before the tragic events of September 11, 2001, that occurred at the former World Trade Center in New York, the Pentagon in Washington, DC and near Shanksville, Pennsylvania. In 2005, the second exercise *Atlantic Storm* was organized around the scenario of a terrorist smallpox attack in Europe.[79]

In 2002, a new Coronavirus arrived from China and caused a SARS corona epidemic, killing 774 people, but it was contained. In 2009, the WHO declared swine flu a pandemic, but it turned out not to be so highly dangerous as originally it was feared it would be. The official death toll worldwide was only 18,449 people. Critics had already pointed out that the WHO, in collaboration with pharmaceutical companies, had exaggerated the danger and spread fear. It was a false alarm. In December 2009, the German physician and politician Wolfgang Wodarg called the false SARS fear campaign "one of the biggest medical scandals of the century."[80] That campaign was an exercise for the next pandemic in 2020.

It is important to recognize that, in 2009, shortly before the swine flu epidemic, the WHO had revised the definition of a pandemic. The WHO at that time defined a "pandemic" as an infectious disease that spreads in several countries in at least two WHO regions, and reference to the severity and lethality of the disease was no longer necessary for the term "pandemic" to be applied to an epidemic. Once WHO officially declared

[78] https://www.centerforhealthsecurity.org/our-work/events-archive/2001_dark-winter/

[79] https://www.centerforhealthsecurity.org/our-work/events-archive/2005_atlantic_storm/

[80] https://www.tagesspiegel.de/politik/gesundheit-schweinerei-mit-der-grippe/1649052.html

a "pandemic," moreover, national health authorities whose nations belong to the WHO were obliged to follow the WHO's rules for dealing with the pandemic. That new definition of the term "pandemic" clearly serves the interests of the pharmaceutical industry. Every new flu epidemic can now be declared a "pandemic." According to WHO rules, sixteen governments bought swine flu vaccines in 2009, which they later had to throw away because the flu virus suddenly disappeared.

Major foundations have also played a role in laying the foundation for the new health dictatorship. For example, in 2010, the Rockefeller Foundation produced the report *Scenarios for the Future of Technology and International Development*.[81] This report presented a scenario called *Lock Step,* which involved a flu pandemic infecting 20% of the world's population and killing 8 million people. It proposed extreme global control measures that were in this scenario most successful in totalitarian China and were implemented in the Corona regime in 2020.

In 2018, the Center for Health Security organized the third *Clade X* exercise, with the scenario of a deliberately created respiratory disease that killed 150 million people.[82] On October 18, 2019, the fourth pandemic exercise, *Event 201*, was held in New York in collaboration with the World Economic Forum and the Bill & Melinda Gates Foundation.[83] It was designed to explore the areas where a severe pandemic would require public-private partnerships to mitigate widespread economic and social impacts. The exercise was attended not only by political leaders

---

[81] www.nommeraadio.ee/meedia/pdf/RRS/Rockefeller%20Foundation.pdf.

[82] https://www.centerforhealthsecurity.org/our-work/events/2018_clade_x_exercise/

[83] https://www.centerforhealthsecurity.org/event201/

and civil servants, but also executives from major companies. The scenario, in which they themselves played the roles, involved a fictional pandemic of a Coronavirus that would kill 65 million people. It raised a lot of suspicion that the Wuhan virus appeared in China a month later.

A biosecurity strategy against the Coronavirus

Bill Gates, having successfully transformed himself from founder of Microsoft to global philanthropist through the Bill and Melinda Gates Foundation, now occupies a prominent position at World Economic Forum meetings and has become the leading force for vaccination as the primary global public health measure. In 2000, he introduced the Global Alliance for Vaccines and Immunization (GAVI) to improve access to vaccination in poor countries. In 2010, he proclaimed the "Decade of Vaccines" at the Forum. In 2015, his foundation invested $53 million in the German company CureVac to develop a new type of vaccine. In 2017, Gates launched the Coalition for Epidemic Preparedness Innovation (CEPI) at the Forum. Its goal is to reduce the time it takes to develop vaccines against emerging infectious diseases from ten years to one year and make them available to developing countries at affordable prices.

The American psychiatrist and well-known critic of psychiatric medication Peter Breggin argues that the foundation of CEPI represents the starting point for the planning of the corona epidemic. This planning "had the dual goals of making money from vaccines, while imposing global governance through an alliance among billionaires, individual countries, philanthropic organizations and corporations – essentially the Great Reset."[84] The Masterplan of Bill Gates for the rapid creation of new vaccines was presented on July 17, 2017, to the WHO. Significantly, at that time there was no documented discussion at the WHO of implementing early treatment for the anticipated epidemic with alternative medications and vitamins.

Since 2013, several pharmaceutical companies have been working on a new generation of mRNA-based vaccines as part of the Fourth Industrial Revolution. Researchers from the Network for Vaccine Research at Imperial College of London presented a report on their work on mRNA vaccines at the 2019 World Economic Forum meeting in the session *Developing a Vaccine Revolution.* It is worthy of note that researchers at Imperial College of London have received tens of millions of dollars in support from Gates, as well as Chinese patrons.

On December 2, 2020, the first such mRNA vaccine, BioN-Tech/Pfizer's Corona vaccine, was licensed for emergency use in the UK. These new mRNA vaccines were approved under extreme political pressure, which has never happened before. The testing and approval procedures, which normally take many years, were reduced to much less than a year, so that we are dealing with a medical experiment on humans in the vaccination campaign. The novel vaccine is to be tested on the entire world population. Such vaccines have not been approved before. According to the latest information vaccine manufacturers cannot be held liable in the event of adverse side effects. Healthy people do not need the Corona vaccine, just as they do not need a

---

[84] Peter R. Breggin and Ginger R. Breggin, *COVID-19 and the Global Predators* (in preparation). Quote from the pdf version of 6.20.21, p. 285-286. Available at https://www.wearetheprey.com/

flu shot. Also, people who had the Covid-19 illness, which made them immune, and children, do not need the Corona vaccine. Nevertheless, it was apparently decided at the World Economic Forum 2020 that such vaccines are intended to be administered to everyone.

Vaccines provoke a controlled infection that stimulates the immune system to produce antibodies. The new vaccines, in contrast, are based on genetic engineering. Vaccination is no longer done with attenuated viruses or a lab-made piece of viral protein, but with active mRNA from the virus, packaged in a shell of nanoparticles. After vaccination, the human cells into which the mRNA is introduced replicate this genetic viral material themselves, which then activates the immune system. The vaccination is in fact a genetic therapy, and it is inaccurate to refer to these substances, other than for convenience, as "vaccines." The human body becomes a GMO, a genetically modified organism. Because the viral material in the vaccine could potentially be incorporated into the cellular DNA, the cellular DNA could be permanently altered. The administering of such vaccines, then, is tantamount to engaging in an experiment with the human immune system without knowing the long-term effects. It is important that an impartial study be carried out to determine the content of the injected substances.

Under the watchful eyes of Bill Gates, the global elite and the WHO, political leaders at the World Economic Forum on January 21-24, 2020, appear to have translated the conclusions of the October 2019 *Event 201* into joint agreements on a strategy to combat the Corona epidemic. Gates and numerous world leaders have framed that strategy as a "war" against the virus. It is an illusion, however, to see the world in terms of being a place where a virus that is spread worldwide can be eradicated. If we compare measures internationally, we can trace them back to a biosecurity strategy with these chief features:

- setting up a global data center;

- introducing Chinese-style lockdowns;

- applying a strategy of fear;

- introducing social distance rules;

- controlling the media;

- taking targeted action against "disinformation;"

- basing guidelines on the PCR test;

- large-scale testing of individuals;

- introducing contact tracing technology;

- vaccinations with the new vaccines;

- indirect or direct compulsory vaccination; and

- introduction of an immunity passport.

When we look at the almost global implementation of this biosecurity strategy, we may identify it as a military operation co-designed by behavioral scientists. The Corona measures can be compared with the methods for enforcing compliance from the Chart of Coercion created by the American psychologist Albert Biderman. They are used to break the will of prisoners of war or to brainwash them. These methods are isolation (lock-down, social distancing), monopolization of perception (media control), humiliation and degradation (mouth caps), exhaustion (daily death reports and ever new virus waves), threats (fines), occasional indulgences (temporary relaxations), demonstration of omnipotence (obligatory tests, etc.) and enforcement of trivial demands (rituals of hygiene, etc.).[85] In the light of these forms of coercion the Corona measures can regarded as psychological warfare aimed at breaking the will of the population. Additionally, spreading lies and fear paralyzes human thinking.

On the eve of the Forum's annual meeting, on January 20, 2020, news spread in Germany that more than 200 people had fallen ill in China. Those reports were immediately followed by a relentless stream of virus-related news worldwide. The WHO began daily reporting on the virus on January 21, and on January 22, the Johns Hopkins Center began registering all cases of the disease in every country in the world on the COVID-19 Dashboard. That information blitz was happening while virtually nothing was known about the Coronavirus.

If one rationally considers all the information that I have provided so far regarding the planning for this "pandemic" that took place years ahead of 2020, it is reasonable to deduce that nothing was left to chance. We can deduce that powerful people on the world stage and the organizations that acted in their interests were eager to declare that the Wuhan Corona outbreak was the epidemic that was feared and promised, and that the innovative vaccine was to be forced on the world as its technological

---

[85] https://niastories.files.wordpress.com/2013/09/bidermans_chart_of_coercion.pdf

fix. In the light of such a deduction, the whole course of events becomes understandable.

The course of the Corona epidemic

On January 22, 2020, a full quarantine was imposed on the eleven million people who live in Wuhan and several other Chinese cities. China reported 444 hospital admissions and 17 deaths. On January 24, WHO reported 25 deaths worldwide. By January 28 of that year, at total of 1,771 new Corona cases had been reported in China. By March 13, there were eight, and then it stopped. According to the Chinese government propaganda, there were no more Corona cases, only normal patients with respiratory illnesses. Chinese authorities attributed their success in containing the outbreak to the Draconian lockdown they imposed on the residents of Wuhan.

On January 30, 2020, the WHO International Health Regulations Committee held a meeting and advised the Director-General to declare a Public Health Emergency of International Concern, which he did. This gave the pharma companies the green light for the development of the new vaccines. Already on January 23, 2020, during the Davos Forum, they had been pressing for such a declaration, but there were not enough cases. A week later there were apparently enough. The development of the vaccines also required the suppression of early home-based treatments, as has been explained by the American psychiatrist Peter R. Breggin: "There is a catch in the federal legislation called the Emergency Use Authorization (EUA) that empowers the government to finance drug company costs for the development of vaccines and to rush them onto the market at breakneck speed without standard FDA approval as safe and effective. Under the EUA, the U.S. could not finance and rush through the experimental and potentially lethal vaccines *unless there were no safe and effective treatments already in place.*"[86]

The five-week lockdown in Wuhan was the first large-scale lockdown in modern times and became a major propaganda success. The Chinese approach to the epidemic was watched with admiration by health technocrats, including the Chinese-backed WHO chief Tedros Adhanom. They proclaimed that we should learn from Asia. This totalitarian lockdown and the other Chinese measures, such as mass testing, became a model for countries where China has influence and were emulated in other countries. Countries that did not want to introduce the lockdown (such as Sweden, Belarus, and Tanzania) were pressured by propaganda from China, the WHO, and the International Monetary Fund, which stopped providing funds. When the German Ministry of the Interior commissioned eight scientists to draft the policy paper that was circulated on March 22, 2020, and became known as the "Panic Paper," two of them were China experts.[87]

The WHO technocratic machine was set in motion in Davos, where the WEF meets. It gained momentum when the first deaths were recorded in Italy on February 22, 2020, and the first quarantine was declared for a still limited area. On March

---

[86] Peter R. Breggin and Ginger R. Breggin, *COVID-19 and the Global Predators* (in preparation). Quote from the pdf version of 6.20.21, p. 24. Available at https://www.wearetheprey.com/.

[87] Aya Velázques, China and The Great Reset, see https://tapnewswire.com/2020/11/how-the-chinese-communist-party-and-western-tech-globalists-sold-the-world-a-lockdown/.

8, the whole of northern Italy was sealed off. In mid-March, television pictures from Bergamo and Brescia were broadcast and caused panic around the world. The medical doctor Luca Speciani from the Bergamo area explained in the summer of 2020 that in those two towns the elderly had received several vaccinations shortly before the onset of their illnesses, which weakened their immunity. Moreover, many Italian COVID-19 patients after their ICU treatment were unwisely brought to care homes of the elderly, where they infected many others.

Medical treatment in Italy for COVID-19 patients was, in a word, disastrous. The Italian media failed to report that the COVID-19 flare-up took place only in those two cities, nor did they report that in Italy such respiratory illness problems occur every flu season and that there was a big staff shortage in the hospitals and care homes. Other factors not considered in media reports were the underfunding of Italian hospitals, and the fact that air pollution in Northern Italy is the highest of Italy. In addition, average age of the Italian population is the highest in Europe. All those factors need to be considered in discussing why an extremely high number of Italian people died at that time.[88] The activities of the Italian media in spreading this alarming COVID-19 news from Bergamo without providing its proper context provide a good example of the staging of media images that have been used in modern politics since 1933 to declare a state of emergency in an atmosphere of public panic. This technique is part of the hybrid warfare of our time.

---

[88] Information presented by Italian experts in interview at www.youtube.com/watch?v=Qm-ls6bj2jxI&t=1119s.

On March 11, 2020, the WHO declared the Corona epidemic a pandemic. That decisive announcement marked the beginning of the collective hypnosis that has robbed many people of their power of judgement. On March 16, Neil Ferguson released his horror scenario of 510,000 dead if the British government did nothing. Around that time most European countries and the United States went into various stages of lockdown. The infection rate had already peaked, but the governments did not know this. As early as March 19, the British government announced that it no longer considered COVID-19 an "infectious disease of major concern." The lethality of the disease was not high enough to merit such concern, they asserted. The British government initially wanted to follow the Swedish example and only introduced the lockdown on March 25, because advisors, the population and parliamentarians had become frightened.

SAGE, the British government's advisory group, included a group of mathematicians who modelled the course of the epidemic. It also included a second group to prepare measures and a third group consisting of psychologists who were to advise on propaganda and manipulation techniques to keep people in fear and make them feel personally threatened.[89] Through the official dissemination of the propaganda they created, and the repetition of lies, over and over again, people started to believe them. A new jargon was developed for the new situation. The people of many countries began to hear in the media the terms "intelligent lockdown," "social distancing" and "the new normal." The last term, by the way, comes from 2004, from a conference on SARS and Bioterrorism.

---

[89] Mike Yeadon, November 2020, www.youtube.com/watch?v=kANkpqtWLN4, between 4:40 and 23:20 min.

By mid-April 2020, it was already clear that the Corona-virus was no more contagious or deadly than other Coronavi-ruses and the usual flu viruses. Israeli health care specialist Isaac Ben-Israel argued in an article published on April 19, 2020, that without lockdowns the Corona epidemic would have been over eight weeks after its outbreak.[90] His assertion was consistent with the standard views on herd immunity, also expressed as we have seen by the American epidemiologist Knut Wittkowski. Nevertheless, many restrictions, which could no longer be justified with medical arguments were not lifted. The resulting damage has been immense. For millions of people, especially children and young adults, the lockdowns are the most dramatic and traumatic events in their lives and affect them for a long time to come. The second lockdowns in the fall and winter of 2020/21 compounded that damage. The additional lockdowns in turn benefited the thriving Big Tech companies, while in Western countries small business is collapsing. Both the big companies and China have a stake in this economic disaster. The Western governments are thereby allowing an economic reset. We are therefore forced to ask them some questions:

- Why should the whole population, including children, be vaccinated? That project will take many months. According to international experts, such as the Dutch virologist Jaap Goudsmit, it would be sufficient to vaccinate only the risk groups. Then the lockdowns could be lifted quickly.

---

[90] www.timesofisrael.com/the-end-of-exponential-growth-the-decline-in-the-spread-of-coronavirus/

- Why are governments not honest about the low risk of Coronavirus, the actual number of COVID-19 deaths (also related to flu), the value of the PCR test, the use of masks, the burden on hospitals compared to previous years?

- Why don't governments allow open discussion with critical experts in the media?

- Why do they allow the psychological, social, and economic chaos in society?

- Why are they using a vaccine against a virus that is not much more lethal than a flu virus, without knowing the long-term effects?

- Why are governments not preparing us for the fact that the Coronavirus, like the flu viruses, will become a part of our lives by providing enough beds in hospitals and supporting the improvement of our immunity through lifestyle changes?

- Why are governments not promoting (instead of discrediting and forbidding!) cheap therapies that can effectively prevent COVID-19 (for example with vitamin D and Ivermectin) and treat it in an early stage? New York medical doctor Vladimir Zelenko, for example, effectively treated many people with a cocktail of Hydroxychloroquine, Zinc and Azithromycin. In 2020 American medical doctor and professor Peter McCullough published as lead author the only two peer-reviewed articles on multidrug outpatient treatment of Covid-19.[91] This treatment led to an 85% reduction in hospitalization, as McCullough testified to the Texas Senate HHS Committee on March 10, 2021.[92]

- Why do governments and religious leaders ignore the spiritual aspects of the occurrence of viruses so that we can learn to understand the message of diseases and especially COVID-19 and change our society to deal with ourselves and nature in a healthy way?

We have seen therefore, and I believe I have summoned sufficient evidence to back up the following assertions, that without a thorough risk analysis of the possible damage to society—in the cultural sphere, in health care, in mental and social life and in the economy—the world's political leaders, under the direction of the WHO, went into an ineffective war against the virus with large-scale lockdowns and border closures. Only a few countries, such as Sweden, deliberately pursued a different course.

Experimental vaccines

The WHO's only exit strategy designed was to stop the virus with a vaccine. This is an irresponsible approach, because viruses mutate all the time, and spread around the world with the flow of people. Coronaviruses cannot be eradicated with a vaccine. They will return every year like all flu viruses. We can expect to see new Corona vaccinations every six months. The protection they give is limited in time (for the Pfizer vaccine the durability

---

[91] www.amjmed.com/article/S0002-9343(20)30673-2/fulltext.

[92] www.youtube.com/watch?v=QAHi3lX3oGM&t=97s.

is six months) and despite having been vaccinated, people can still be infected by the virus, get ill and spread the virus to others, with the same level of transmissibility as the non-vaccinated. The vaccination only seems to prevent a dangerous infection, while growing numbers of vaccinated people are hospitalized due to the less virulent and less dangerous Delta variant of the virus, as data from Israel show, where a third vaccination is taking place.

To understand the nature of mRNA vaccines and the alarming situation around the present vaccination program, two videos can be recommended. The first one is a presentation given on August 10, 2021, by Robert Malone, the American vaccine specialist, and the original inventor of the mRNA vaccine technology in the late 1980s.[93] The second one is a medical report on the current state of affairs concerning the negative effects of the experimental vaccines, presented by Ryan Cole, M.D., from Idaho on August 11, 2021.[94]

Dangerous allergic reactions, brain thromboses and other health problems, sudden deaths, long term adverse effects occurred in many people after vaccination with the mRNA (Pfizer and Moderna) and the vector-based vaccines. Those cases are only partially reported, and the true numbers of such cases will never be fully known. The Vaccine Adverse Event Reporting System (VAERS), a US national vaccine safety surveillance program co-sponsored by the Food and Drug Administration (FDA) and the Centers for Disease Control and Prevention (CDC), already reported a massive increase in deaths in the first four months of 2021 related to the vaccination program.

---

[93] https://rumble.com/vl0zpf-dr.-robert-malone-the-liberty-forum-8-10-2021.html.

[94] https://www.youtube.com/watch?v=tUE5EBPt-lU.

In these months alone, VAERS has received over 40% of all death reports it has ever received in its entire 30+year history.[95] Between December 14, 2020, and July 2, 2021, VAERS received 9,048 reports of death and 438,441 adverse events among people who received a COVID-19 vaccine.[96] It was said that review of available clinical information has not established a causal link to COVID-19 vaccines, but this raises questions on their causes and on non-reported cases.

There are obviously many reasons to be critical of the use of vaccines, and especially so of the new type of vaccines developed against Coronavirus. A recent series of news items reported on an investigation of the anti-vaccine information circulating on social media. Those reports claimed that 73% of the anti-vaccine posts and tweets on Facebook from February 1 to mid-March 2021 originated from the same twelve sources: "Those 12 sources, which the report calls the *disinformation dozen,* are: Joseph Mercola, Robert F. Kennedy Jr., Ty and Charlene Bollinger, Sherri Tenpenny, Rizza Islam, Rashid Buttar, Erin Elizabeth, Sayer Ji, Kelly Brogan, Christiane Northrup, Ben Tapper, and Kevin Jenkins." The report complained that "the majority of the disinformation dozen remain on major social media platforms, despite repeated violations of their terms of service."[97] It is well known that the pharma industry discredits people who bring the research of independent experts to the public.

Based on information revealed by such expert research-ers, it is reasonable to expect uncontrolled autoimmune reac-

---

[95] https://principia-scientific.com/the-deadly-COVID-19-vaccine-cover-up/ (May 13, 2021)

[96] https://www.cdc.gov/coronavirus/2019-ncov/vaccines/safety/adverse-events.html

[97] https://www.self.com/story/vaccine-disinformation-on-social-media.

tions of the immune system among people who have received the new vaccines, especially older people. The German cell biologist Vanessa Schmidt-Krüger warned of the dangers of the nanoparticles in the BioNTech/Pfizer vaccine as early as December 2020.[98] The Canadian professor of viral immunology Byram Bridle gave his critical comments on questions related to the vaccinations and herd immunity on February 24, 2021. In his view, people who already have a natural immunity should not be vaccinated. For him, the Corona crisis is "the greatest mismanaged crisis of our time."[99]

On March 7, 2021, Belgian vaccination research expert Geert Vanden Bossche wrote an open letter to the WHO warning that global vaccination will turn "the rather innocent virus into an uncontrollable monster" because it will create more infectious mutations. He also fears that with mass vaccination during an epidemic our natural innate immunity will be weakened in its activity.[100] Others are speaking out as well. The German lung specialist Wolfgang Wodarg is one of the most important independent experts. In a recent article on his blog he reported on March 15, 2021, on the dangerous side effects of the Corona vaccinations.[101]

Wodarg also pointed out that the antibodies produced by the body to destroy the cells infected with the mRNA might also attack the body's own protein syncytin-1 and lead to infertility

---

[98] Two videos at: www.youtube.com/watch?v=xLx2yJAmqdU and www.youtube.com/watch?v=oNGFXiBVV8M.

[99] https://dryburgh.com/byram-bridle-coronavirus-vaccine-concerns/

[100] https://dryburgh.com/geert-vanden-bossche-open-letter-to-who-halt-all-COVID-19-mass-vaccination/

[101] Blog of Wolfgang Wodarg, www.wodarg.com/english/

in vaccinated women. This protein is necessary for the implantation of a fertilised egg. In a petition they sent to the European Medicine Agency on December 1, 2020, Wodarg and Yeadon requested the immediate suspension of all SARS-CoV-2 vaccine studies, to address the various safety concerns.[102]

The new vaccines are genetic therapies, not classical vaccines, and for this reason their emergency use authorization would have required long-term studies of genotoxicity (the toxicity of the injected substances) and biodistribution (their distribution in the body). Dr. Robert Malone alerted the American Food and Drugs Administration (FDA) that these studies had been neglected and that the spike proteins in the vaccines were in fact dangerous and toxic to cells. The pharma companies and the FDA officials were aware of these risks, according to Malone.[103]

A Harvard study published on May 20, 2021, showed the circulation of spike proteins in the blood of vaccinated nurses as early as day 1 after the first vaccine injection.[104] A biodistribution study of the Pfizer and Moderna vaccines sent to the Japanese health authorities showed that a certain amount of spike proteins got into the ovaries, adrenal glands, heart, brain, liver, and other tissues of rats at 48 hours following the injection. Also, the lipids (the "envelopes" of the spike proteins in the vaccine) spread all over the body, 12% of them in the ovaries. The injected substances do not stay in injected area, as had been expected.

The facts concerning the adverse events raised serious questions among an international group of 27 experts, who in a

---

[102] On their petition see: www.regulations.gov/comment/CDC-2020-0121-0181.

[103] https://www.youtube.com/watch?v=Du2wm5nhTXY.

[104] https://academic.oup.com/cid/advance-article/doi/10.1093/cid/ciab465/6279075.

petition of June 1, 2021, urged the FDA against a premature full approval of COVID vaccines.[105] This should wait until necessary efficacy and safety studies are completed and substantial evidence would demonstrate that the benefits of an individual COVID-19 vaccine outweigh the harms. This requires studies that must address the following concerns:

- Coagulopathy issues, including blood clots, haemorrhage, thrombocytopenia, heart attack, and strokes.

- Reproductive issues, including menstrual irregularities, reduced fertility, miscarriages, and preterm births. The vaccines induce the generation of antibodies to attack spike protein, which are genetically like proteins produced by the placenta.

- Carcinogenesis. There is preliminary and theoretical evidence that the spike protein may promote cancer.

- Transmission of spike protein (or its fragments) from vaccinated individuals, such as through breast milk and associated risk in neonates and infants.

- Neurological disorders.

- Cardiac issues, including myocardial infarction, myocarditis, and pericarditis.

- Autoimmune diseases.

---

[105] https://www.regulations.gov/document/FDA-2021-P-0521-0001. In spite of this petition the Pfizer vaccine received the full approval of the American FDA on August 23, 2021.

On July 17, 2021, Malone spoke about three "noble lies" (lying in the interest of the common good) which leading politicians and health officials have used to show a way out of the crisis:

1. We must reach herd immunity to get out of the crisis.

2. We reach herd immunity **only** through universal vaccination.

3. Vaccines are completely safe and provide protective and durable immunity.

That these "noble lies" are false is now breaking through the censorship.[106] There are effective drugs, the vaccinations do not lead to herd immunity (nor lasting personal immunity), passing through natural infection is the usual way of reaching herd immunity (and lifelong personal immunity), and there are too many adverse events to call the vaccine safe.

In another interview Malone stressed the importance of the principles of bioethics in administering experimental vaccines. They include openness concerning all the risks, explaining them in clear language, and voluntary participation. These principles are violated, Malone states, because laypeople do not know the risks and are put under pressure, at the same time that adverse events are underreported while governments continue to declare the vaccines safe. In many countries governments make the vaccination mandatory for certain professional groups and limit the rights of non-vaccinated people. At the end of July 2021 President Biden declared all federal employees must receive vaccination or submit to regular testing. He even requested

---

[106] https://newsvoice.se/2021/07/dr-robert-malone-current-covid-crisis/

local authorities to give people $100 for their vaccination, and Walmart wanted to offer $150 to its employees. According to the bioethical code of Nuremberg, minors should not participate in medical experiments, but governments also intend to vaccinate them, even in some jurisdictions without their parents' consent.

It is too soon for me to express an opinion on reports coming from Spanish researchers Dr. José Luís Sevillano and Ricardo Delgado, part of a group calling itself "La Quinta Columna" ("The Fifth Column"), to the effect that graphene oxide has been found in the Pfizer and Moderna vaccines. One significance of this discovery, if confirmed as true, is that the graphene oxide is conductive to electricity, which would be a factor in explaining the reports that come people are experiencing parts of their bodies that received the injections are becoming magnetic. There are numerous videos online with these gentlemen talking about this matter in detail.

It should be noted, however, that Karen Kingston, described by journalist Stew Peters on his video show as a former Pfizer employee, also has a great deal to say about graphene oxide inside mRNA vaccines. Although it is likewise too soon to comment on this information, it deserves study. [107]

There are plans to digitally record vaccinations in an online immunization record. The public-private consortium ID2020 has been working on that project since 2016. This digital health identity is a global project. The German government wanted to introduce an immunity passport in May 2020, but after much protest, the government's proposal was withdrawn—temporar-

---

[107] https://tapnewswire.com2021/7pfizer-whistleblower-confirms-toxic-graphene-oxide-inside-mma.jab

ily. In May 2021, the European Union decided to introduce a vaccination passport to "facilitate" summer travels. In addition, a technique has been developed to place a digital mark on the skin when vaccinating with infrared dye, which can be read with a scanner.[108] Such products are examples of the new technology of the Fourth Industrial Revolution.

The outbreak of the Corona epidemic in China in January did not look dramatic at first. Nevertheless, the German virologist and government advisor Christian Drosten, who must be considered a representative of the pharmaceutical industry, worked with a team on a PCR test based on the Chinese analysis of the Coronavirus genome, which has been available since January 10, 2020.[109] The test was ready on January 16, 2020, and was recommended by the WHO as a standard test for all laboratories in the world. Test kits were produced immediately. On January 21, the scientific paper on the test was submitted to the journal *Eurosurveillance* and accepted just one day later.

Although this test is not intended for diagnosis, but rather to support a previous medical diagnosis, as its inventor Kary Mullis repeatedly said,[110] it serves as a basis for government policy internationally. On November 27, 2020, an international group of experts led by the Dutch molecular geneticist Peter Borger called for the article to be withdrawn because of serious

---

[108] See for these *Quantum-dot tattoos*: https://stm.sciencemag.org/content/11/523/eaay7162.

[109] It is repeatedly claimed that the Chinese have already isolated and displayed the complete genome. However, that claim cannot be confirmed. We still need to question if the isolation of the sought-after Coronavirus has not yet taken place in its entirety. That question raises other questions on the link between a not isolated and not fully sequenced Coronavirus and the disease, as the American medical doctors Tom Cowan and Andrew Kaufman do. See https://andrewkaufmanmd.com/sovi/

[110] www.youtube.com/watch?v=ClqxbvwVGYU

errors that rendered the test useless.[111] On February 5, 2021, there was a response from the journal's editors, who rejected the retraction request without addressing the criticisms. This can be described as a scientific scandal.

In many countries citizens demonstrate against the totalitarian measures and lawyers go to court. From July 2020, the German Corona Committee holds weekly hearings with experts on the relevant aspects of the Corona epidemic.[112] Those hearings have given rise to an international group of lawyers who started class action lawsuits in Canada and the United States against those responsible for the introduction of the PCR test. Their work takes place in cooperation with the work of Robert F. Kennedy Jr.'s Children's Health Defense organization, a non-profit group dedicated to disseminating information about the dangers of vaccination and promoting a healthy environment. When Kennedy, a professional attorney, was in Berlin, Germany on August 29, 2020, he gave a famous speech in support of what was probably the biggest demonstration in German history. He made the following statements: [113]

"We want health officials who don't have financial entanglements with the pharmaceutical industry—who are working for us. We want officials who care about our children's health, and not about pharmaceutical profits or government control. . . The governments love pandemics. They love pandemics for the same reason they love war. It gives them the ability to impose controls on the population that the population would otherwise

---

[111] https://cormandrostenreview.com/report/

[112] The videos of these hearings are available at: https://corona-ausschuss.de/

[113] https://www.youtube.com/watch?v=zfe__wsmvSY

never accept—creating institutions and mechanisms for orchestrating and imposing obedience. . . And the pandemic is a crisis of convenience—for the elites who are dictating these policies. It gives them the ability to obliterate the middle class, to destroy the institutions of democracy, to shift all of our wealth, from all of us, to a handful of billionaires to make themselves rich by impoverishing the rest of us."

Government leaders are responsible for setting up a health dictatorship to save their underfunded health system. The many billions of dollars and euros in damage that this dictatorship has caused worldwide could have been better spent on improving health care. The political leaders should have cancelled all measures after three weeks, when it became clear that the Coronavirus is no more deadly than the flu viruses. Instead, they used useless PCR tests to declare people infected and to quarantine them and the people they were in contact with. Such restrictions also affected the staff of hospitals and care homes. As a way out of this problem, we are told, everyone is to be subjected to a vaccination experiment.

Resistance to the health dictatorship

The lawyers working with the German Corona Committee under the able leadership of Reiner Fuellmich and many others are preparing to bring suits in courts around the world, alleging that the actions of governments in implementing the Corona health policies were criminal acts. I believe that in time the historical record will declare them to have been exactly that.

In her book *The Shock Doctrine*, Canadian journalist Naomi Klein described how governments use (or manufacture) crises to carry out their long-prepared control plans.[114] Health technocrats have taken the threat of the Corona epidemic to gigantic proportions with a non-diagnostic test to put society into a state of shock that must last until everyone is vaccinated. They do so mainly in the interests of the pharmaceutical industry, but also of the big corporations that want to implement the innovations associated with the Fourth Industrial Revolution. Materialistic science wants to create total control over humans, society, and nature.

With their PCR tests and their model-based expectations, the health technocrats have constructed a pseudo-reality in which everything revolves around the mysterious Reproduction number "R," which is based on assumptions. For them, dealing with the Corona epidemic is a technical problem, not a human one. Many people who uncritically believe what political leaders claim cannot imagine that governments lie and act criminally. They therefore prefer to assume that the virus is mortally dangerous for most people, although we have known since April 2020 that this was not the case. Those who openly observe what is happening now and see how lies rule can look with great concern into the future of our society and our humanity. The totalitarian world state under Anglo-American control with disempowered subjects, which has been prepared for more than a century as the New World Order, has now come to light with Chinese support in the global health dictatorship.

---

[114] Naomi Klein, *The Shock Doctrine*, Penguin, Harmondsworth 2008.

The planned technological Great Reset, modelled on China and its technocratic social credit system under total surveillance, will fundamentally change our society and our humanity—but only if we let it happen.

We can summarize the ascent of the health dictatorship in the following steps that have been described by the French historian of health Patrick Zylberman in 2013 and applied to the situation of 2020/21 by the Italian philosopher Giorgio Agamben:

1. The construction of a fictitious worst-case scenario.

2. The adoption of this worst-case scenario as the basis for health policies.

3. Enforcing the compliance of the population to government measures.

Agamben spoke of an experiment in which a new paradigm of governance is designed "whose efficacy will exceed that of all forms of government known thus far in the political history of the West".[115] This is one of the ways in which the New World Order is taking shape that will end the age of liberal democracy.

---

[115] Giorgio Agamben, Biosecurity and Politics, May 12, 2020, at https://non.copyriot.com/biosecurity-and-politics/. See an interview with him from August 2020 at https://www.youtube.com/watch?v=867_5upU55o.

The New World Order

Until the First World War, Great Britain dominated a large part of the world. One can therefore speak of a British world order which, after a transitional period, changed into an American world order in 1945. To actualize that order, new institutions were created at the end of the Second World War. Those institutions were the International Monetary Fund and institutions later called the World Bank and the World Trade Organization. In addition to this new economic infrastructure of the world order, the United Nations was founded as the nucleus of a world government. All those developments were under American control.

The American world order, of course, did not and does not encompass the whole world. It did not include the Soviet Union with its satellites and allies. Since 1989, Russia, like China, has followed its own course, although they are members of Western institutions. Since 1979, the West has actively supported China's economic development. It is now the emerging world power. America is still the leading power militarily, politically, and economically. However, the economic elites who own the international corporations with their money include wealthy people from all parts of the world.

Informally, the British and American elites have worked together since the First World War in the areas of economics, politics, and the media to align their interests. Before that time, masonic lodges played a role as a network of mainly European elites and intellectuals. After the Second World War, their place was taken by other groups. The best known is the Bilderberg Group, co-founded in 1954 by the Dutch Prince Bernhard van Lippe-Biesterfeld. Representatives of the American and Western European elites were able to meet under the aegis of that organization. In 1973, on the initiative of the American banker David Rockefeller, the Trilateral Commission was founded, comprising American and European as well as East Asian business and political leaders, especially from Japan. Much has become known about the origins and methods of the Trilateral Commission, which openly works toward one world government and owes its political ideology to the Technocracy movement of the 1930s, through the ground-breaking research of Patrick Wood and Antony Sutton in 1979 and 1980.[116]

The Bilderberg Group and the Trilateral Commission are not secret societies, but closed circles in which world problems are discussed and a common strategy is sought. The main goal in the background is a world government, as David Rockefeller stated on several occasions.[117] The names of the members of these elite circles are available for those who wish to do the necessary research. The World Economic Forum, founded in 1971 as the

---

[116] Patrick Wood and Antony Sutton, *Trilaterals over Washington*, Mesa (AZ) 2017.

[117] One of the statements is from 1991, at https://www.goodreads.com/author/quotes/9951. David_Rockefeller.

European Management Forum, was initially aimed primarily at the European business community. Since that time, it has become an annual meeting place for the world's leaders, including, as I have mentioned, leaders of the Chinese elites. To this large network of global elites, we can add the hundreds of think tanks and research institutes where academics explore global problems and strategies in the service of the elites.

There has long been talk of a new world order. After the First World War, the American President Woodrow Wilson spoke about it. He referred to the fundamentally changed balance of power in the world. After the Second World War, it was talked about again and after the end of the Cold War, the American President George Herbert Walker Bush spoke of a new world order on September 11, 1990. After the two world wars, the elites were again striving for a world government. Conversations about this movement in academia or think tanks for decades were marginalized, as the mainstream press and many political leaders considered the "new world order" a "conspiracy theory." The project of the Great Reset, presented in 2020 by Klaus Schwab, however, made clear that the centralization of control on a global level by the elites has been a long-prepared pre-pandemic plan.

After the failed wars in the Islamic world and the rise of China, the end of the American world order is in sight. Perhaps we are dealing with a 72-year historical rhythm. Just as communism collapsed 72 years after the Russian Revolution of 1917 in 1989 due to the upheavals in the Eastern Bloc, 2017 marks 72 years since the end of World War II. In that year, Donald Trump became President of the United States. With his slogan *"America first,"* he seemed to have assumed the role of gravedigger of the Western world order. America should look after itself, he asserted, and not the world. Despite Trump's efforts to put America first, the fact remains that the peoples of the world are in a transitional phase towards a multipolar world order in which not only the United States, but also the European Union, China and other major countries are responsible for the political situation in the world. In this utterly new world order, the biggest companies from the West and China will be dominant. We may expect them to attempt to organize the world according to the Chinese totalitarian model.

While major corporations will naturally play a leading role in this effort, it is important to understand the complex agendas of the United Nations and the organizations it spawned. Created in 1945 under American leadership and largely financed by the United States, with its headquarters building in New York City erected on land donated by the Rockefeller family, the United Nations has long had a positive image through the work of one of its agencies, UNICEF, which initially worked to improve living conditions for children in developing nations. It is important to realize, however, that the World Health Organization is also a spinoff of the United Nations, established in 1948 to pursue the laudable goals of identifying global public health issues, coordinating public health activities, and promoting the health of the world's population.

As we have seen, the WHO has lived up to its mission under the aegis of the UN and has played the role of the international coordinator of the Corona epidemic. It is not so well known by the world's population, however, that the WHO's role in "promoting global health" is in turn part of a larger agenda, the global sustainable development agenda. The Great Reset must be understood in terms of that agenda, as well.

The concept of "sustainable development" originated in a 1980 United Nations report. In 1987 the *Brundtland Report* defined it as "development that meets the needs of the present without compromising the ability of future generations to meet their own needs." The UN leadership took a new step in 1992 at the Earth Summit in Rio de Janeiro, where Agenda 21 for the 21st century was drawn up. That agenda is all about people, the planet, prosperity, peace, and partnership. As a further step toward "sustainable development," the UN's Agenda 2030 was formulated in 2015 with 17 Sustainable Development Goals to be achieved by 2030.[118]

On the surface, all the goals of sustainable development, which promise major progress in education, health, care of the environment, food production, etc., are highly praiseworthy. A closer look at the literature, and at the actions of governments already at work to implement the goals of these agendas, reveals that the entire field of sustainable development has been hijacked by international corporations that dominate the world order. In all areas of development, scientific and technical plans are drawn up, brought in by consultants and monitored bureaucratically, yielding profits for Western corporations. This work is happening systematically in the developing world, but also in the western world. It is in the work of so-called sustainable development that we can see the technological reset of the World Economic Forum at work. We will examine this work and its impacts in the areas of food production, education, health care and climate.

---

[118] https://en.wikipedia.org/wiki/Sustainable_Development_Goals.

Control of food production

Changes in the global food supply provide a very vivid example of the takeover by big corporations in all areas of sustainable development. The Indian activist Vandana Shiva has been denouncing this takeover for decades. With other Indian leaders, she founded the organization Navdanya in 1986, which campaigns for biodiversity, organic farming, farmers' rights, and the protection of seeds. After initially working to organize opposition to the biochemical company Monsanto and the leading food multinationals, Navdanya published the report *Gates to a Global Empire*, about the activities of the Bill & Melinda Gates Foundation, in October 2020.[119] In this foundation Bill Gates, who at 31 became the youngest billionaire in history, concentrated his philanthropic activities in 1999. Shiva has become world famous for denouncing Gates and his philanthropic activities as "philanthrocapitalism," especially in her most recent of many hard-hitting books, *Oneness vs. the 1%*.[120]

The *Gates to a Global Empire* report shows that the leadership of the Gates Foundation is not interested in developing truly sustainable and inclusive agricultural models, but in consolidating the model of intensive industrial monocultures for the benefit of the large-scale seed and agrochemical industry. Together with international companies trading in genetically modified seeds, Gates is involved in the complete reshaping of food production in Africa and India. They hold patents on seeds and the genetic codes of stored seeds from all continents, which they genetically modify. The Gates Foundation is a sponsor of CGIAR, the largest

---

[119] https://navdanyainternational.org/publications/gates-to-a-global-empire/

[120] Vandana Shiva, *Oneness vs. the 1%*, New Internationalist Publications, Oxford 2019.

agricultural innovation network. In January 2020, the foundation established a new subdivision, Bill & Melinda Gates Agricultural Innovations, to make "scientific breakthroughs" available to smallholder farmers in Africa, Asia, and Latin America.

The Gates Foundation advances its interests in many areas by investing money in research, universities, start-ups, development programs and projects, and the media. From 2001, Gates sponsored the International Alliance for Improved Nutrition, which promotes biotechnologically "improved" food. In 2006, he launched the Global Development Program, which gave birth to the Alliance for the Green Revolution in Africa.

On November 9, 2020, an article was published in which Vandana Shiva gave her opinion on the Great Reset.[121] She noted, "The Great Reset is about multinational corporate stakeholders at the World Economic Forum controlling as many elements of planetary life as they possibly can." She added that it is about "maintaining and empowering a corporate extraction machine and the private ownership of life." A partner of the World Economic Forum is the Swedish Food Forum EAT, founded in 2014. Its mission is to change the global food system on a scientific and sustainable basis. It uses food developed in laboratories, such as "cultured meat," an artificial "meat" grown from cell cultures. Healthy foods linked to regional diversity are thus, if the EAT initiative succeeds, to be replaced by genetically modified foods.

The co-founder of the EAT is the Wellcome Trust, which is intricately linked to the pharmaceutical industry. On the Plan-

---

[121] Jeremy Loffredo, 'World Economic Forum's 'Great Reset' Plan for Big Food Benefits Industry, Not People', in: *The Defender*, 9. November 2020.

etary Food Diet proposed by the EAT, Shiva remarked, "The diet proposed by the EAT is not about nutrition at all, it is about big business, and it is about a corporate takeover of the food system. . . The EAT's uniform global diet will be produced with Western technology and agricultural chemicals. Forcing this on sovereign nations by multinational lobbying is what I refer to as food imperialism."

The charitable work of Bill Gates' and other billionaires' foundations, such as the Carnegie, Dell, Ford, Rockefeller foundations, is not altruistic. With their money, they create knowledge and policy networks in which the interests of technology companies, scientific institutions, governments, and subsidiaries of the United Nations are aligned. In these networks, goals are set, policies are formulated, projects are prepared, indices and metrics are determined to measure the degree to which goals have been achieved, and registration systems are developed to record everything. In practical implementation, we see technocrats and managers at work everywhere who are not controlled by democratic institutions. People like Bill Gates and the heads of the big companies behave like a *de facto* world government. National governments are becoming the enforcers of their policies.

Control of education

Another area of change is education. Since 2000, the competencies of 15-year-old students have been regularly tested in the Programme for International Student Assessment (PISA), a worldwide comparative study organized by the Organization for Economic Co-operation and Development (OECD). In 2004, the adoption of the Dublin Descriptors launched a European education policy with final performance levels for colleges and universities. As a result, higher education is increasingly geared towards meeting international technocratic standards. Schools prepare and select young people for the international labor market and the Fourth Industrial Revolution, instead of supporting the development of their creative potential and the qualities they need as articulate citizens. The digitalization of education, including in primary school, makes learning outcomes even more measurable. At the international level, this digitization has been launched by a network of representatives from UNESCO (United Nations Educational, Scientific and Cultural Organization), education ministers, producers of learning programmes, think tanks, consultants, and foundations, such as the Gates Foundation. School computers are sponsored worldwide. The journalist Whitney Webb has done an excellent job of describing this development in a highly detailed essay *From UNESCO Study 11 to UNESCO 2050*.[122]

In 2020, digital education has received a new push as in-person education was blocked in schools in many countries. For example, numerous major corporations and institutes founded the Global Education Coalition on March 16, 2020. Among its founders were the big profiteers of the closures, including Microsoft, Google, and Facebook, plus the BBC, McKinsey, IBM, the Johns Hopkins Institute for Education Policy, and representatives of the Global Business Coalition for Education, which had been working on this project since its founding in 2012.

---

[122] unlimitedhangout.com.

Control of health care

As we move toward synthesizing all the information presented in this book, it is important to examine a little more closely the role that Bill Gates plays in healthcare and vaccine development, to which I have referred earlier.

We should take into consideration that Gates is no newcomer to this field, as he has primarily focused his philanthropic work and vast fortune on "global health" since the early 1990s. In 1999, he established a Malaria Vaccine Initiative with $50 million to develop a vaccine against malaria, which is still not available today. He also supported the International AIDS Vaccine Initiative with $25 million. At Gates' initiative, the Children's Vaccine Initiative, founded in 1990, was transformed into the Global Alliance for Vaccines and Immunization (GAVI) in 2000 to improve access to vaccination (against childhood diseases, yellow fever, hepatitis B and the H influenza viruses) in poor countries. GAVI brings together governments of developing and donor countries with WHO, the World Bank, the vaccine industry, research institutes and private philanthropists. Gates launched the rebranded GAVI at the World Economic Forum's 2000 meeting, where he pledged $750 million to fund its work.

In 2010, Gates proclaimed the "Decade of Vaccines" at the meeting of the World Economic Forum. At the end of 2010, the WHO declared that it would create a global action plan for vaccination together with the Gates Foundation. In 2017, the Coalition for Epidemic Preparedness Innovation (CEPI) was launched at the World Economic Forum in Davos. The initial investment of $470 million was provided by a consortium of several countries and sponsors, including the Bill & Melinda Gates Foundation. As I mentioned earlier, at the 2019 World Economic Forum, three prominent scientists from Imperial College's UK Vaccine Research Network presented "the next generation of vaccines." They are the so-called vaccines that are now available for use against Coronavirus.

With the decision by the Biden administration to resume funding for the WHO, the Gates Foundation is one again WHO's second largest sponsor after the United States. In 2018/19, this contribution amounted to 9.4% of revenue. Thus, Gates and the institutions and multinational companies associated with his foundation continue to exert a major influence on the policies of this organization. Through his work, he presents himself as a benefactor of humanity. China contributes much less, but with the decisive Chinese votes, the current WHO top man Tedros Adhanom was appointed to lead the organization as its Director General.

The leadership of the WHO wants to increase its control over global health issues. In May 2020, the WHO created an Independent Panel on Pandemic Preparedness and Response. The panel published its first report in May 2021, called *COVID19: Make it the last Pandemic*. The first of the four recommendations read that the "WHO [establishes] a new global system for surveillance, based on full transparency by all parties, using state-of-the-art digital tools to connect information centers around the world and including animal and environmental health surveillance, with appropriate protections of people's rights."[123] The report praises the countries which engaged in the most authoritarian "anti-COVID" measures, specifically China and New

---

[123] COVID19 Report, p. 53, at https://theindependentpanel.org/

Zealand. In effect, it is promoting centralization, globalization, and totalitarianism as elements of a global biosecurity state.

Climate control

The issue of climate change has been on the United Nations agenda since the *Earth Summit* in Rio in 1992, where the first international environmental treaty was concluded. This was followed by the Kyoto Protocol of 1997 and the Paris Climate Agreement of 2016. Measures to protect the climate are part of the Sustainable Development Goals. There is little controversy about whether the climate is changing, as new temperature records are constantly being measured and ice caps and glaciers are melting, but there is controversy about the scientific models used. The main question is to what extent CO_2 emissions are responsible. The treaties have chosen to reduce greenhouse gas emissions, with a system of carbon credits. This requires a complex transition to non-fossil energies led by international companies and the introduction of a CO_2 tax under technocratic control. Geoengineering experiments are also underway, which are described in the mainstream media as aimed at reflecting solar radiation back and affecting the climate.

Bill Gates is a co-sponsor of the Stratospheric Controlled Perturbation Experiment (Scopex), which planned to conduct an experiment in Sweden in June 2021 using scattered lime at an altitude of 20 km to reflect solar radiation back into the cosmos. After protests from several environmental organizations the Swedish Space Corporation decided In April 2021 not to conduct the planned test flight.

Other authors, though, such as Elana Freeland, state based on their research that "geoengineering" also involves the spraying of the atmosphere with toxic electro-conductive substances such as aluminium, strontium and barium. Its goal is the creation of a medium for the transmission of highly charged ions for the purpose of altering the weather and creating a conductive medium for radio-controlled long-distance drones and other surveillance technology.[124]

The question that is not asked here is to what extent our economic system of unbridled growth and energy waste, which is not questioned in the technocratic plan of the Green New Deal eco-dictatorship, can still be linked to the proper treatment of the earth. This question takes on another dimension when we see the earth as a sacred and living organism with which we have lost the inner connection, as the American researcher Charles Eisenstein described in his book on climate.[125] This connection existed in all traditional cultures, through our Western materialistic thinking in recent centuries.

According to the World Economic Forum, the problem of climate change is even bigger than the Corona epidemic. If we do a reset now, we could better address the climate problem, believes Klaus Schwab. Because US President Trump pulled out of the climate agreement in 2017, the planned reset could not take place then. The Coronavirus offers a new opportunity. Trump, whose re-election was not desired by the elites, is now out of the picture.

---

[124] Elana Freeland, *Chemtrails, HAARP, and the Full Spectrum Dominance of Planet Earth,* 2014 and *Under an Ionized Sky,* 2018, both published by Feral House, Port Townsend (WA).

[125] Charles Eisenstein, *Climate – A New Story,* North Atlantic Books, Berkeley 2018.

The lockdowns are driving the global financial system, which has been completely unstable since 2008, into even deeper trouble due to the rising debt burden of almost all countries. Klaus Schwab does not write about this, but there has long been talk of a new global monetary system led by the IMF, in which the US dollar loses its central position. Such a monetary reset remains in the background but could unexpectedly become a reality. The first step would likely be the abolition of cash by central banks and the transition to digital money. The ticking time bomb of the bankrupt financial system is for now out of our consciousness. When the crisis of the monetary system comes, the Coronavirus may conveniently be identified as its cause.

We can now summarize the rise of the New World Order as the attempt to create biosecurity (health control), climate control, control of education, mind control, cyber control, food control, human reproduction control, control of social unrest, and money control by the elites and their technocrats. This is the creation of a global pyramid of power.

The Pyramid of Power

In the reset planned by the Davos elite, democracy, to the extent that it still exists, will be replaced by an oligarchy (rule of the few). The ideal of democracy as a form of government in which the people (in ancient Greek: *demos*) exercise power has its origins in Greek culture. That ideal stands in stark contrast to the despotic forms of government of ancient Persia and Egypt, in which an autocrat exercised power. Greek democracy was quite limited, however, as women and slaves were not counted as part of the people. Only free men with property could participate. That was also the practice of American democracy, which emerged after the adoption of the Constitution in 1787. Only white men who had some property (usually land) had the right to vote, until suffrage was extended to all citizens in the twentieth century.

The justification for that restriction was seen in the protection of the property of the wealthy, who feared that their wealth would be distributed among the population if everyone were allowed to vote. When Western countries introduced universal suffrage a century ago, the rich had the same problem. If the poor came to power through socialist parties, laws could be passed that could end the privileged position of the rich through nationalization or high taxes. These wealthy people were no longer just the landowners and merchants of older times, but also the owners of factories and the bankers who looked after their money.

The rich have always looked for ways to control the masses. To help them, willing scientists developed psychological and social techniques that could play on people's fears, shape public opinion through media propaganda techniques, and manipulate their needs through marketing techniques.[126] By naming or creating enemies, such as terrorists, the people united behind the leader. All these techniques accompanied the development of democracy. Moreover, the powerful in society knew how to use political parties for their own purposes. Democracy as the power of the people is thus an illusion. Instead, one must speak of a plutocracy, the rule of an elite of rich people.

After the Second World War, the elites were willing to pay high taxes to repair the war damage, but also because of the social contract between labor and capital. This contract gave rise to the welfare state with all its social services. From 1980 onwards, the social contract of the welfare state collapsed under neoliberal policies. Tax rates were lowered, and companies and the rich avoided paying taxes to an ever-greater extent. Organized labor lost more and more influence and governments had to go into debt to make ends meet.

---

[126] Edward Herman and Noam Chomsky, *Manufacturing Consent*, New York 1988. Noam Chomsky, *Media Control*, New York 1991, the documentary *Manufacturing Consent*, 1992, and *Propaganda and The Control of the Public Mind*, Cambridge (Mass.) 2001. See also the British television documentary series *The Century of the Self*, made by Adam Curtin in 2002 at www.youtube.com/watch?v=eJ3RzGoQC4s.

The rich of our time make their money in the form of returns on invested capital deployed by the managers of modern corporations. Those corporations are in many cases more powerful than governments, especially in the emerging sectors of the Silicon Valley Big Tech sector and social media, telecommunications, pharmaceuticals, and biotechnology. Through lobby groups, the big corporations exert influence on government that does not inherently serve the interests of the people. They can use the money to sponsor political parties, open-up careers for former politicians or put their own people in high positions in the government apparatus. This direct power of international business is known in America as corporatocracy—the rule of corporations. The European Commission tries to limit the power of big business in Europe but does little more than impose fines for harming competitors.

Technocracy

Modern society has developed its own form of government, which we find in politics as well as in business. This is technocracy, first described in the French philosophical tradition of the early 19th century. Count Saint-Simon defined it as the management of things, which would replace the rule of people. Human decisions would then become superfluous because everything could be handled administratively according to certain rules. The French philosopher and sociologist Jacques Ellul, in his important 1954 book *The Technological Society*, defined "techniques" as the rational and efficient methods used in every field of human activity to make social relations, political structures, and economic phenomena manageable. He saw Western societies as inevitably moving toward the conditions we now know, and call "technocracy."

Several precursors of modern technocracy emerged during the 20th century. In the Soviet Union it emerged as Marxism-Leninism through the 1917 revolution against the Tsar staged by the Bolsheviks and went into full force under Josef Stalin. Interestingly, in the decisive year of 1933 the world witnessed both the installation of National Socialism in Germany under Adolf Hitler and the New Deal national economic planning policies of President Franklin D. Roosevelt. Today, in different variations, we see centralized power subjecting the whole of society to rules and degrading people to objects of state power. The state now interferes in all areas of society.

Our technocratic societies are the modern version of ancient Egyptian society, where the pharaoh was at the top of the power pyramid, and his powers were distributed through a hierarchical structure of priests and scribes who oversaw every aspect of Egyptian life. Over time, the nature of power has changed. In Egypt power was essentially religious; in the Roman Republic and medieval empires it was primarily political; and in the last century economic considerations have come to dominate the use of power. The big corporations impose their will on the state and eliminate the input of the people. They are focused on maximizing profits, but rules are needed to regulate the world market so that the big players have a framework within which to operate.

The Great Reset starts with the big corporations. They are concentrating their power at the top of global society in the form of a world government where, under their supervision, the institutions of the United Nations, the United States and the European Union create frameworks within which they can protect their interests. Such concentration of power is made possible also through trade agreements that give them the right to sue states whose political decisions harm their economic interests. National politicians are the enforcers of their wishes and secure the cooperation of the population. In national parliaments, citizens' rights are still rarely weighed. Policies set at the international level are further elaborated at the national legislative levels. Technocrats at all levels work to create rules. At international conferences, non-governmental organizations representing civil society are the interlocutors who are supposed to speak on behalf of the people but are rarely effective.

The big international companies are in fact corporate states, and their power is greater than that of most countries. They behave as if they are above the law. Time and again there are scandals that show they are breaking national and international laws. In some cases, such as in the Big Tech industry, an industry is allowed to regulate itself and then immoral violations of privacy occur. The fact that financial interests take precedence has led to rampant white-collar crime. We all know the most common examples of such crimes from the headlines in recent years: car companies faking emissions tests; banks selling worthless mortgages; pharmaceutical companies marketing vaccines that have not been properly tested; chemical companies producing carcinogens and poisons that wipe out insects; agribusinesses driving small farmers into the abyss; telecommunications companies setting their own radiation standards for mobile phones and wireless connections without health testing; tobacco companies adding substances that make smokers addicted; Big Tech companies developing programs with addictions deliberately built in, such as computer games. The list is almost endless. We are dealing with modern corporate mafias that have no respect for human dignity and freedom, poison the environment, plunder the earth, and disrupt the natural balance. We are also aware that vast criminal organizations in many countries are seemingly beyond the reach of law enforcement and have now taken root in many countries, dealing not only in drugs and rare earth minerals, but in human lives as well.

In the field of public health in relation to the Coronavirus, we have seen how, under the auspices of the WHO, measures have been taken at the world level that have very rapidly led to the global health dictatorship. Those so-called public health measures are no longer about people's health and survival, but about the subjugation of society to a totalitarian regime that serves the interests of the pharmaceutical industry. This vision of global society and the treatment of individual rights can be seen in all areas where international companies operate and can make money from us. They force us to work for them as "wage slaves," just as in ancient Egypt and other ancient autocracies everyone worked for the pharaoh. Now we work to buy products that make big profits and that in many cases we do not even need.

A society of free citizens

This view of the human being as a slave to totalitarian control must be contrasted with the great project of modern culture that has been at play in the world for at least the last five centuries. I would describe that project the creation of a society of free people who develop spiritually, who regulate their mutual relations based on equality, who work together in solidarity for the common good and who treat the earth responsibly. Human freedom is, of course, limited by natural conditions, by our environment and by forces that we are not always free to deal with, such as fears, addictions, and prejudices. Through the development of culture, however, we can learn to deal with and transform those limitations. Through the ethical use of scientific knowledge, we can change natural conditions, and through education we can develop inner freedom. Working on ourselves can help us overcome our personal problems. A society in which culture becomes entertainment and education leads to a one-sided upbringing allied with the new technocratic agenda, however, keeps us trapped within our limitations.

The pyramid of power in which control over our lives increasingly shifts to the top of global society is the legacy of ancient cultures in which people were much less individualised than today and did not yet have independent control over their lives. At the end of the Middle Ages, societies of free citizens emerged, as in the Italian city states, the Swiss cantons, the trading cities of the North and the Republic of the United Netherlands. Here the pyramid of centralized power was gradually turned upside down, so that power came from the citizens rather than from the church or the nobility. The American Declaration of Independence confirmed this new role of the citizens. This development was countered by the rise of the modern state on the one hand, and the large international corporations on the other. The centralization of power and the disempowerment of citizens represent a major step backwards towards collective consciousness and the loss of individual freedom.

That such large concentrations of power have occurred in politics and the economy is also the result of a lack of consciousness among citizens. Modern political leaders who represent the interests of the rich elites know how to manipulate the population and thereby secure these interests and their own careers. Thus, the shadows of ancient Egypt and ancient Rome hold us in their grip. Leaders with moral consciousness, who also exist, are being tested to see if they remain true to their ideals. Everywhere people are awakening, working from ideals towards a world in which a new political consciousness overcomes the social forms of the past.

There are other reasons why the multinational corporations and the billionaires' foundations have become so powerful. Corporations have evaded paying taxes on a large scale. In addition, since 1980, in the era of neoliberalism, tax rates have been lowered and the corporations have had a decisive influence on government policy since the Second World War. The concentration of power of international corporations has been made possible by money that would otherwise have been used for public purposes through taxation under democratic control.

We are now faced with the question of how to use modern technologies. The Davos elite are doing a reset for the benefit of the world's powerful people. Their spokesmen, who represent the political elites, are using a new slogan for this reset: *Building back better*, by which I believe we can assume they mean "the better rebuilding of global society." They are using the self-inflicted Corona crisis to gain more control over the people. It is a matter of great concern that such people are now praising the concentration of power in the totalitarian Chinese society, where the government has set up a social credit system using facial recognition and artificial intelligence in a society where surveillance is total and absolute. In this system, citizens who do not play by the rules lose points, so they ultimately may lose the ability to travel or practice their profession.[127]

The emergence of such a surveillance state in Western countries, accelerated by the Corona measures, is provoking resistance from many people.[128] Big business, international organizations and the emerging world government need to be monitored and corrected. Such mechanisms of correction, though, are missing. It is already a problem that the European Commission can only be controlled to a limited extent by the European Parliament. The countervailing force must come from society. Direct democracy is the means to this end, and it can be implemented with the help of modern technology. It is time to restart the move towards freedom, which is at the heart of European and American culture. People must not be manipulated and subjected to propaganda. We are by nature creative beings who can shape our own lives.

It is sometimes assumed that citizens are not capable of making judgements about the problems of today's complex society. The proper exercise of citizenship requires articulate citizens, and a political organization of society where legal issues are transparent. Those are issues that affect everyone and on which everyone should have an equal say in their capacity as human beings. They include laws that define rights and duties and the organization of society. The task of citizens in political

[127] See the report *China's Digital Dystopian Dictatorship* at https://www.youtube.com/watch?v=eViswN602_k.

[128] Shoshana Zuboff, *The Age of Surveillance Capitalism*, New York 2019.

life is to determine framework conditions within which people can develop freely, in which their rights as human beings are guaranteed, and in which they are not embroiled in a struggle for existence but can use the natural resources for a humane society in cooperation with each other. This requires a different reset than the World Economic Forum wants to implement with its top-down approach. The changes must come from the grassroots, from the citizens and not from elites pursuing their own interests. How to shift power from the top to the grassroots of society is the topic of the next chapter.

The Humane Future of Society

In our thinking about society, we may have to leave behind some basic ideas that prevent us from renewing social life. Such ideas, for example, include the following concepts: we live in a democracy; the government cares about the common good; the free market and competition are good for the economy; government institutions should work like a business; the media are independent; education should be adapted to the needs of business, etc. Such thoughts cloud our picture of social reality because we can question every such assertion.

We need some key ideas that can be understood by any thinking person. We can start from what the World Economic Forum presents in its reset as a caricature of the humane society of the future, enforced with even greater force than has been the case since the breakthrough of neoliberal policies in 1980. In this reset, a world designed by the biggest corporations appears. With psychological and social techniques, and the media, politicians manipulate the population to accept this design. For this purpose, scientists provide new technologies making society controllable, promising huge profits to the rich, creating a culture of permanent entertainment and enabling virtual connections, but not actual encounters, between all people through social media. In this technological "paradise," where everyone can live "sustainably," the well-being of all humanity would presumably be served.

In such a society of technology and control, our lives will be determined by invisible elites. Aldous Huxley (*Brave New World*), George Orwell (*1984*), Yevgeny Zamyatin (*We*) and many others have written eerie novels about this nightmare, which is also the theme of many films. What we need are creative thoughts to build a free society together. We will then be able to discuss fundamental issues that are no longer debated in parliaments or in the election campaigns of today's societies. The introduction of 5G, technological innovations or Corona measures are decided by the elites, as I have discussed, at the meetings of the World Economic Forum in Davos and on other related occasions and sites.

Instead of a society ruled by the financial and economic elites with the help of their political friends, we can imagine a society that realizes, at a higher level, the democratic traditions of the village communities of earlier times. This, I suggest, must be a political order in which every person has an equal voice and in which elections are free, fair, and legitimate. "We the people" no longer need political parties that divide the population according to the Roman principle of "divide and rule" and in many cases are corrupted by economic interests.

Such a new political order requires grassroots democracy in which decisions are made at the grassroots of society. Such an order can be achieved through various forms of direct democracy, such as the referendum. A new form of governance that fits such an aim is the citizens' assembly, which already has a consultative function in many cities and countries. Here citizens who form a representative cross-section of the population come together for a few days to form a common opinion on a political problem with the advice of experts, starting from the question of what is fair for all.[129] In this way, political awareness is created.

We can look at a few examples of such assemblies that are starting to emerge:

- "California Speaks" was a statewide deliberative forum on health care reform that took place on August 11, 2007, in eight counties. Nearly 3,500 people representing all segments of the population were randomly recruited to participate in a day-long discussion of health care reform proposals that were before the California legislature.

- The "Citizens' Initiative Review" is Oregon's version of an assembly. A panel deliberates on a ballot initiative or referendum to be decided in an upcoming election. The number of participants is around two dozen. They are often paid for their time and travel.

- The "Washington Climate Assembly" was the first state-wide climate assembly in America. It took place in 2021, gathering seventy-seven randomly selected citizens to discuss climate change. Their recommendations were brought for consideration to the State Legislature.

---

[129] https://en.wikipedia.org/wiki/Citizens%27_assembly.

- It is also worth noting here that author Dr. Naomi Wolf, long an activist for women's issues and on the increasing trend to totalitarian government in the US and other countries, has recently become an outspoken critic of official COVID-19 policies, forced vaccinations and vaccine passports. Remarkably, although she is a former advisor to former President Bill Clinton, she has been speaking out on conservative media outlets, as she apparently no longer welcomed in the mainstream US media. Most significantly, she has also become the CEO of a new company designed to make it easier for ordinary American citizens to get involved with the legislative process in their states and in the federal government, which can be found at DailyClout.io. Daily Clout also has a Facebook page, a podcast, and a YouTube Channel, and is emerging as a very useful tool for people who want to go beyond attending rallies and writing letters to their congress members and senators.

To keep political decisions close to the people, the principle of subsidiarity must be consistently observed. Such a principle means that decisions must be made at the lowest level and may only be delegated to a higher level if this is not possible at the lower level. Such a practice allows for decentralized government where there is now a trend towards a superstate. The trend to centralization needs to be reversed. The delusion of a superstate stems from the belief in the power of the state bureaucracy to order society from a central point. This is the French idea of the social-technical society, which also flourished under socialism in many countries until it finally bankrupted itself at the end of the Soviet era.

This idea of the value of centralization underlies all technocratic thinking, which is always making authoritarian plans, creating policies in accord with those plans, and implementing them. This rational thinking has led to the government interfering in everything, even in matters that would be better left to the representatives of culture and the economy. In most modern societies, government technocrats for example control education, right down to its content, and at ever higher levels experts set the standards that education in Europe and other parts of the world must meet. This control extends to all areas of society, and governments thus appropriate competencies that lie in these areas to themselves.

Thus, here a *first* key idea can be formulated that concerns political life: Politics is about shaping social life in which all people have an equal voice as responsible citizens. The implementation of such a key idea requires a small-scale approach and decentralization. It also requires the development of a culture that turns people into responsible citizens instead of independent cogs in a large technocratic apparatus. We ourselves must shape the political and legal framework in which we want to interact with each other, and which is presently imposed from above in our technocratic society.

In recent decades, we have lived in a caricature of a creative culture. In a truly creative culture, though, we develop our consciousness and our spiritual life, our gifts, and talents. We thereby become human beings in the truest sense of the word. We can call this self-realization. This educational process should continue in education and lead to the skills that make us people with critical thinking skills and responsible citizens, and that enable us to respond to what other people need. A culture that only provides entertainment creates people without imagination who can no longer think.

Culture should enable us to discover truth through thinking. In the age of fake news and "alternative facts," many people lose faith that the truth about something still exists or is accessible to us. Truth thus becomes opinion. This makes us vulnerable to manipulation, we no longer think about what we hear, and we can easily become victims of propaganda. The result is that the official news about the Corona epidemic is no longer exposed as a half-truth or a lie by many people, especially those who feel vulnerable and afraid.

Culture is no longer autonomous because the interests of the economy have permeated it. Culture must generate money, or it will be cut back. Most culture is sponsored to raise corporate profile. Education likewise is being forced to meet the demands of the economy, so its formative role is disappearing. In schools, knowledge and historical awareness are declining, even literacy, numeracy, and correct writing. With the increase of internet courses in schools and universities, the teacher or lecturer can no longer fulfil an inspiring and motivating role. Scientific research is increasingly subordinated to the interests of the clients who provide the money. The reset of the World Economic Forum will lead to an even stronger link between science, technology, and international business. Research that falls outside the purely materialistic framework in which everything is reduced to material causes will no longer be able to be funded.

Technologists want to make us more intelligent by connecting our brain to a computer. However, a computer has a highly restricted form of intelligence. It is a strictly logical thinking that distinguishes between yes and no, 0 and 1 in computer language, and it needs electricity. A computer can only do what it has been programmed to do. Human intelligence is infinitely more comprehensive. It includes intuition, inspiration, and imagination, it can develop into wisdom and can be guided by our moral sense and creativity. Living intelligence, which according to American psychologist Howard Gardner has eight dimensions, is reduced to abstract, schematic, dead, non-moral, non-creative thinking by our use of computers.[130] The merging of our brain with a computer is the opposite of what many cultures strive for as a cultural ideal, namely the connection of the head with the heart, which is the seat of wisdom.

We can now formulate a *second* key idea for the development of culture: People must be able to develop freely. For that purpose, money must be available, which should come as an endowment from the economy. In a free cultural life, the capital of the future is formed, which as human talents and abilities helps society to progress. Every form of influence and programming undermines human dignity.

The economy that developed after the Middle Ages was based on competition. This was justified in the 19th century with reference to the theories of Charles Darwin. He claimed that there is a struggle for existence in nature that leads to the survival of the fittest. Darwin's point of view was a one-sided perspective. Other biologists, such as the Russian Pyotr Kropotkin, saw the

---

[130] Howard Gardner, *Multiple Intelligences*. Basic Books, New York 2006.

principle of mutual cooperation at work in nature, which is also present in human coexistence. The reality of aggression cannot be denied, but the purpose of culture is that we learn to deal with it. Modern entrepreneurs often still must learn to cooperate with each other, but also with their employees, consumers, suppliers, and society, to recognize their common interests.

The world of international corporations is a world of war, resulting in the elimination of competitors and small producers everywhere, the establishment of monopolies, and the burdening of society with external costs such as damage to the environment and the earth. The rich elite want to receive dividends and higher shareholder value. Most wars are fought over access to resources, such as oil in the Middle East or rare earth minerals in Africa. This is a system that is not sustainable but is fuelled by greed for money.

In ancient societies, the economy was at the service of culture. The surplus of the harvest was not only exchanged with others, but also used to support priests, healers, and singers. In some tribes, such as the Kwakiutl Indians of the Pacific Northwest states in the USA, people who had surpluses would organize a potlatch feast for the whole community to consume the surplus together and distribute needed goods. In the great empires of antiquity, especially in the Middle East, debts were cancelled after every war, famine and change of throne. People who had become slaves were set free again. Such practices prevented an army commander or a high official from whom loans had been taken from becoming more powerful than the king.[131] In our

---

[131] Michael Hudson, *And forgive them their debts,* 2018, and YouTube videos.

time, we have failed to cancel the debts of the poor, and so the rich have become richer and richer.

In the process, markets for labor, property and capital emerged, tearing society apart. Peasants became wage laborers who had to sell their labor (instead of the products of their labor), common land was appropriated by the powerful, and money enabled bankers to create money, which was not the original function of money at all. Kings and local lords in the Middle Ages put only money into circulation that was backed because it had a value in silver or gold, or because the local lord had enough grain in his stores that could be bought with his local tin coins.

In our current monetary system, banks have the right to create money. They only need a small part of their own capital to create credit. In this way the money supply is continually increased, and money is continually reinvested to produce new profits. As a result, money has an eternal life, while it must also "die" to keep society healthy. This dying of money can take place by no longer investing or sending it, but by gifting it to culture so that individuals can develop their talents. In the application of their qualities thus acquired, new capital is created. For a healthy society, it is necessary that the banks lose the right to create money, so that money can be created in society altruistically, for the common good.

A levy could be paid for the use of land by farmers and entrepreneurs, which would be available to the whole community living in a certain area or country. In 2018, the already mentioned Dutch researcher Rutger Bregman spoke of a citizen's dividend that would benefit everyone equally. Such a dividend could be financed from the use of the commons, including land, the common natural basis of our existence, which should not be privately owned. This land rent should not be distributed by the state and can be made available to residents in various ways. In this way, culture can be funded, and everyone can have equal access to it.

This is not the world that the elites envision. They want control over the whole earth, all resources and everyone's labor force. In our society, we work primarily to earn an income, not because others need the products of our labor. We can also reverse this perspective and build an economic life in which we work for others and develop an awareness of the people who work, in the production chain, for our needs. That reversal would be an economic life based on real demand for products and not on products for which artificial demand is created through marketing and advertising. Such a new economy would be based on cooperation between consumers, producers, and the intermediaries, and on a fair price that includes all costs, including those of damage to nature.

These considerations lead to the formulation of a *third* key idea for a healthy economy: By working together and in solidarity, we share the fruits of the earth and make our interdependence visible.

We can now contrast these three core ideas with the goals of the Great Reset:

- Freedom in culture versus control over our thinking.

- Equality in politics versus technocratic decision-making.

- Solidarity in the economy versus exploitation by the rich.

Can we realistically put these three core ideas into practice? It is not possible in a society where we do not give each other space, space to develop in culture, space to have a voice in political life, space to get what we need to survive in the economy. In our modern society, this space for the other has become smaller and smaller and the space we individually claim for ourselves has become larger and larger. This new vision is possible in a society where we realize that we are interdependent. Then, instead of extreme individualism, we can develop a social consciousness in which there is room for everyone.

Such visions were developed by people who understood that each generation owes its existence to previous generations and to the infrastructure built up by society. Such visionary people also understood that no one should rule over others without a mandate to do so for a certain time, and that we cannot do without each other. We need new ideas for the future of our society. Some such ideas for a new society have been with us for a long time but have increasing relevance in our times.

For example, the scholar and mystic Rudolf Steiner, the founder of Anthroposophy, developed a vision in 1917 for a society in which cultural life is organized according to the principle of freedom, political life according to the principle of equality, and economic life according to the principle of fraternity. Culture, politics, and economy are the components of a "trisector" or "threefold" society.[132] Created during the tremendous devastation created by the Great War, what we today call World War I, Steiner's vision for a new society was intended as a peace

---

[132] Harrie Salman, *The Social World as Mystery Center*, Threefold Publishing, Mountlake Terrace (WA) 2020.

program. In this vision, education and health care should not be controlled by the state, but by independent civil society organizations. It was also intended by Steiner to prevent Germany and the countries of Eastern Europe from becoming part of the new Anglo-American world hegemony. As we know, his vision tragically never came into being as Germany marched into the disasters of National Socialism, and the world was engulfed, in only two decades, in another tragic world war.

Europe has become part of American world hegemony. The Great Reset will bring us even further under the control of the global elites. To free ourselves and those whom we love from the prospect of such dark future, a different kind of reset is needed. How are we going to do that?

What We Can Do

The lockdowns have completely unbalanced our society, even more than it already was. For many, this is also true in their private lives. The planned Great Reset could make this even worse. Therefore, activity is required from us. Groups of friends are doing research together to find more information, discover how our world is really run and what interests are behind the scenes. We can raise questions, discuss with each other what is good for us, make conscious choices, and create the communities out of which a new society of free and brave people will develop. With the Corona epidemic, we live in a new reality where lies rule. Governments always tend to misrepresent what they do to justify their policies. Corporations do not disclose their intentions and the quality of their products. This situation forces us to study the reality we live in and share our findings with others, but also to take concerted action with others. This situation also applies to the way we spend our money, because that is how we steer the direction of production in the economy.

Creating a healthy social life

There are major tasks to be done to steer our societies into a direction that corresponds to the consciousness of independent people who do not want to be slaves to the economy, dissatisfied citizens in politics, or complacent enjoyers of entertainment in culture. In each of these areas, the right balance has been lost. Science, politics, and economics are dominated by control, violence, and war. Those are "masculine" qualities that have become extreme because they are not humanised by "feminine" qualities. Economic interests dominate culture and politics. Between economy and culture, the harmonizing middle of a political life is necessary, which orders our society out of the interests of the citizens. Inequality between rich and poor is increasing, also on a global scale. In individual life, the balance between head and heart, intelligence and emotion, work, and leisure, sitting and moving, talking, and singing, money and well-being, the material and the spiritual aspects of life has been lost. The result is that so many people have health problems. This is not a purely individual problem, but also a societal problem. Our society is sick and needs healing. The Great Reset will not bring healing, but more control over people.

Spiritual impulses are needed to heal individual and societal illnesses. The sources of healing lie in the higher consciousness of the individual. A century ago, Rudolf Steiner brought with Anthroposophy impulses for healing for the individual and for all sectors of society. In all countries of the world, people have developed new ideas and visions. One of them who deserves to be mentioned is the Croatian-Austrian priest, philosopher and social critic Ivan Illich (1926-2002), whose books on compulsory school education, medicine and the "war against subsistence" waged against peasant societies anticipated the total loss of our autonomy that we are facing now in the Great Reset.[133] We can work with the healthy, uplifting forces of body, soul and spirit, and with the forces of nature. We can reshape the small world around us with more social awareness. Everyone can create a free space for research and judgement, determine rules and make decisions on an equal footing with others, and practice solidarity with others in a new economic life.

Fruitful interaction with each other is a social art. Conflicts with others show that we still have much to learn. Conflict inevitably happens in our relationships, our groups, communities, and organizations. What we learn in our relationships can help us understand the dynamics of the larger society. Empowered people do not allow themselves to be manipulated and do not allow power to be exercised over them without their consent. Such empowerments require agreements. When people talk to each other, they need to make inner space and practice empathy for each other. In any social context there must be a power-free space where rules can be made together. In society, this is the sphere of politics, where rights and duties are agreed upon and society can be organized. We learn to be responsible citizens by political action, by standing up for ourselves, by claiming our rights, but also by recognizing the rights of others.

---

[133] Ivan Illich, *Deschooling Society* (1972), *Tool for Conviviality* (1973) and *Medical Nemesis* (1975).

Creating a new healthcare system

We need medicines that have no side effects and that cure chronic diseases. The products of the pharmaceutical industry make diseases manageable, but do not cure them. The industry continuously earns money from chronic diseases. For modern medicine, the human being is a biochemical machine that can be repaired with chemicals, implants, stem cells and new organs. Iatrogenic damage caused by doctors and their expensive medical interventions is a major cause of death. Antibiotics are prescribed far too easily, making hospital infections a disaster in many countries. Painkillers like oxycodone and fentanyl are responsible for tens of thousands of deaths in the United States every year.

Health care should not be controlled by state authorities and a health technocracy that serve the interests of Big Pharma, but by independent civil society organisations in which representatives of patients and medical doctors are in charge. In the European Union, the pharmaceutical industry is pushing off the market anthroposophical and homeopathic medicines, plus other natural remedies, claiming they have no scientific basis. Such medicines, however, have no side effects and have been used successfully for over a century. Nature has its own pharmacy. We can familiarize ourselves with herbs and other healing substances from nature and use them and consult with qualified holistic practitioners. Those who live and eat healthily can rely on the wisdom of the body.

The doctors and other professionals who practice standard health care have great faith in vaccines but do not know in general how to influence the human immune system in a healthy way. Such people and industry spokespeople keep silence about the side effects of vaccines and see to it that opponents of vaccination are ridiculed. Many books critical of vaccination are now published and available.[134] In the United States, Robert F. Kennedy Jr., and his organization Children's Health Defense have for many years been suing the pharmaceutical industry for the damages its products cause to people.[135] Kennedy speaks of the totalitarianism that has resulted from the *coup d'état* perpetrated by the big pharmaceutical companies and the big tech companies. As I have demonstrated throughout this book, Corona vaccines are a new generation of vaccines whose long-term effects we simply do not know. We must defend our bodily autonomy and integrity against mandatory vaccinations. Moreover, we must reconsider, with the American medical doctors Zach Bush, Tom Cowan and others, the theory of contagion according to which viruses cause diseases, against which we are told by authorities that we must be vaccinated.[136] Such a reconsideration of the "germ theory" could lead to a new paradigm of natural immunity, a new concept of health and mental wellbeing.

Instead of propaganda for vaccination, we should be given information on how to strengthen our immunity. Our immunity has physical, individual, and social aspects and a relationship with living nature. On a physical level, we should have unpolluted air, live a healthy life, eat a whole food diet, and take vitamins. Zach Bush has shown the dependence of our immu-

---

[134] Thomas Cowan, *Vaccines, Autoimmunity and the Changing Nature of Childhood Illness*, Chelsea Green Publishing, White River Junction (VT) 2018.

[135] https://childrenshealthDefence.org.

[136] For a general analysis see Zach Bush in conversation with Del Bigtree at https://zach-bushmd.com/video/the-highwire/. Thomas S. Cowan and Sally Fallon Morell, *The Contagion Myth*, Skyhorse Publishing, New York 2020.

nity on healthy food and healthy soil.[137] On an energetic level, nature provides additional life forces when we walk outside, enjoy nature and sunlight, which provides the very necessary vitamin D, of which so many people are deficient. The German doctor Thomas Hardtmuth states that a daily walk in the forest of one hour increases the function of our immune system by 50%. Whether we get sick depends primarily on our organism and not on the virus, says Tom Cowan.[138] As individuals we can control stress and learn to cope with it, sing and play music, get enough sleep, overcome our fears, protect ourselves from negative forces and radiation, live in harmony with ourselves and get excited about what we find important. In our social life we give each other life forces by meeting each other, hugging each other, singing with each other, experiencing joy and being constructive and supportive of each other. It is an incredibly sad situation that everything the government asks of us in its Corona strategy of fear has a negative impact on our immunity.

There is natural electricity and magnetism, but also technologically generated electromagnetic radiation, which can be very harmful to humans. When electricity reached the American Indian reservations, the Indians found that their connection with living nature was lost. Electromagnetic fields intervened. In the 20th century, researchers discovered the connection between the emergence of new uses for electricity and the appearance of new diseases. The American researcher Arthur Firstenberg documented this in a ground-breaking book.[139] Electrosmog takes many forms, as radiation from electrical appliances, mobile

---

[137] www.youtube.com/watch?v=0WT3dcz4QIU, 2021.

[138] Thomas S. Cowan and Sally Fallon Morell, *The Contagion Myth.*

[139] Arthur Firstenberg, *The Invisible Rainbow – A History of Electricity and Life*, London 2020.

phones, antennas, smart meters and 5G (with the thousands of satellites it requires). The "safe" limits have been set by the companies themselves. The dangers are well known to telecom companies and governments, as described by Canadian ex-electronic warfare specialist Jerry Flynn.[140] Independent research into the effects of electrosmog has almost never been considered, despite the steadily increasing number of electrosensitive people. In some countries the roll-out of the 5G network has been halted, but we hear nothing about it in the press. This new network has been hailed by governments, without citizens having a say, as an innovation project they need for crowd control and other technological innovations. The continuing roll-out of 5G since 2019 may have even made people more susceptible to COVID-19, as the leading 5G researcher professor Martin Pall argued.[141] It is important to note that Wuhan in China was the world's first 5G smart city. There is now a wealth of independent research on the effects of electromagnetic fields, mobile phones, Wi-Fi, smart meters and 5G on the health of people, animals, and nature.[142] Active citizen resistance is needed to protect us against these effects, which may be more serious for our health than global warming.

Caring for body, soul, and spirit

Much of our modern food is factory food with added chemicals and too much saturated fat, salt, and sugar. As a result of

---

[140] Jerry G. Flynn, *Hidden Dangers*, Bowser (BC, Canada) 2019.

[141] Martin S. Pall, Argument for a 5G-COVID-19 epidemic causation mechanism, March 20, 2020, https://electromagnetichealth.org/

[142] See the scientific research of Martin S. Pall on the risks of 5G: https://peaceinspace.blogs.com/files/5g-emf-hazards--dr-martin-l.-pall--eu-emf2018-6-11us3.pdf

chemical agriculture, our food is low in minerals, low in vitality, contains residues of agricultural poisons, pesticides, toxic metals and, in the case of animal foods, hormones, antibiotics and microplastics. The agroindustry modifies the genes of food plants and has them patented. Genetically modified food has no nutritional value compared to natural and organically grown food. Animal meat will be replaced by meat from laboratories in the future. Many people in the world are now returning to natural foods and a healthy diet.

Chemistry is poisoning people on an unprecedented scale. Such poisoning not only has physical consequences, but also puts a strain on our mental and spiritual functions. According to the holistic physician Dietrich Klinghardt, practicing in Seattle, our spirit is driven out by the calcification of the pineal gland (epiphysis), located in the center of the brain. According to him, aluminum, found in vaccines and distributed in the atmosphere by geoengineering, glyphosate in food and in the air, from the herbicide Roundup and fluorine in our water are mainly responsible for this calcification. The pineal gland is the most sensitive part of the central nervous system and is sensitive to those toxins. Wi-Fi and 5G radiation (especially the 2.4 GHz wavelength) open the blood-brain barrier, allowing them to reach this gland, which according to ancient lore receives higher spiritual energies and is the seat of the soul. Such exposures to toxic chemicals and radiation render the human spirit ineffective.[143]

Our soul needs protection from the abundance of sensory stimuli that come at us in the world of technology and from the

---

[143] Dietrich Klinghardt, Video *Light vs Dark, Heavy Metals & Toxins*, 2019, with recommendations for detox: www.youtube.com/watch?v=zR6OiKNnp2M.

one-sided materialistic and un-artistic education of our time. Thinking, feeling, and willing are functions of the soul that are exercised by our ego. Freedom of thought is under pressure in our society because free thoughts are dangerous for the interests of the ruling elites. In the inner space of our soul, we experience ourselves and the outside world. With our will we give shape to our lives. Nevertheless, the development of our souls is in danger. Rudolf Steiner foresaw in 1917 that a vaccine would be produced to manipulate the body as soon as possible after birth so that the human being would later no longer think there was a soul, a spirit. The materialistic doctors will drive out the spirit. The inclination to spirituality will be driven out in earliest childhood by a vaccine, he predicted.[144] We can imagine that toxins in vaccines and the manipulation of the immune system are responsible for this.

A German study founded on anthroposophical spiritual research explained that the coronavirus and the spike protein injected with the "vaccine" have the physiological effect that they attack the physical foundation of the spiritual function of thinking. Knowing that the coronavirus is the result of genetic manipulation we may consider that the virus and the genetic therapy developed to "protect" us represent an attack on the core of our spiritual being, as predicted by Steiner in 1917.[145]

Care of the soul was one of the motivations for the development of philosophy. Human consciousness has grown over

---

[144] Rudolf Steiner, lectures of October 7 and 29, 1917: *The Fall of the Spirits of Darkness* (Collected works 177). https://www.rsarchive.org/GA/index.php?ga=GA0177. See also: Daniel Hindes (ed.), *Vaccination in the Work of Rudolf Steiner*, Aelzina Books, Longmont (CO) 2021.

[145] Elaim Gairo (a pseudonym), *COVID 19 – Die globale Seelenentfremdung*, Verlag Vier Himmelsrichtungen, Reichenwalde (Germany) 2021.

the centuries, but large parts of our subconscious are still not accessible to consciousness. This is the field of psychotherapy, which enables us to become aware of the forces at work there. We carry shadows in our soul that can take possession of us, such as fears and unconscious desires. They can be awakened and manipulated through propaganda and advertising techniques. There are beings working in the subconscious that are known in all spiritual schools of inner development. They need to be neutralized and transformed. Such forces and beings also work in groups and in all of society, manifesting as nationalism, racism, and other collective fears. In addition to the unconscious, our soul also includes the superconscious, both on an individual and collective level. From this we get our inner images, inspirations, and intuitions.

Through our spiritual development we become more aware of our ideals and the power we possess to work with them. Our minds need challenges where they have been dulled in our culture, and an upbringing and education that stimulates and awakens our spirit. The materialistic visions that prevail today deny the spirit and even the reality of the soul. We need our spirit to transform society so that we can live in it with dignity as free human beings. The result of this would be the creation of a network of parallel societies in which a healthier way of life and a more intelligent way of using technology are able to germinate for the wellbeing of humanity.

Epilogue: The Choice between Two *Zeitgeists*

In his famous novel *The Brothers Karamazov* (1879-1880), the Russian writer Fyodor Dostoevsky included a story about the Grand Inquisitor of Seville. He describes how Jesus visits Seville, where several thousand people were burned by the Inquisition in the 16th century. Jesus resurrects a dead child and is captured by the almost 90-year-old Grand Inquisitor to be burned at the stake the next day. The inquisitor visits Jesus in his cell and tells him that people who receive enough food are willing to give up their freedom for it. They also give up their moral judgement and are easily dominated. He reproaches Jesus for having died on the cross to redeem people who do not want to be free and are willing to submit to the church and the state for bread. Jesus makes no reply, kisses the inquisitor, and walks out of his cell.

The leaders of the new world order are taking away people's freedom and moral judgement and offering them "bread and games" in the form of industrially produced food and internet entertainment. They are doing so in an increasingly totalitarian world, in which our health will be permanently monitored, food production is in the hands of bio-tech multinationals, digital education suits the desires of business, and a carbon climate dictatorship is coming. The designers and administrators of the Fourth Industrial Revolution are working hard to make such a dystopia inevitable. Through that revolution, they intend to transform us into bio-machines, a combination of a human being and an intelligent computer, as envisioned by prominent transhumanists such as Ray Kurzweil and Elon Musk.

In their vision, human beings of the future will no longer have an ego, a spirit or a soul, or their own thoughts, emotions or free will. Human beings will be genetically modifiable and programmable and can be manufactured in the laboratory with a genetic design for specific tasks. Through the Internet of Things, human beings will be integrated into a world-wide system. Society as we know it now will no longer exist. It will be one big machine, which will also include animate nature and the climate. In our time, society is already largely run by technocrats as a socio-machine. The Corona measures will further destroy society as a whole organism of living, human relationships. The Great Reset, if we allow it to operate without opposition, will continue this work.

Here we see essential symptoms of the illness of our society. The elites make use of their power to create societies in which people have lost their autonomy in the areas of the mind, their constitutional rights in politics and their sense of mutual solidarity and connectedness with nature in economy. This thinking and acting in term of domination and control characterizes modern science, politics, and economics. The ideas behind the Great Reset will only strengthen the existing mechanisms of power and control over human beings and nature. The war against the Coronavirus is a product of the same attitude. We create an artificial world, instead of relying on natural processes, balances, and harmonies. Freedom, equality and solidarity and respect of nature disappear. To heal our society, we need to reverse the pathological developments of modern social life and to transform these pathological ways of behavior in ourselves. Instead of domination we can develop a life of partnership with others, serving, caring, and creating harmony.

Medieval society with its ecclesiastical power apparatus had inquisitors to suppress people's freedom. Modern society has its technocrats to maintain the pyramid of power and eliminate people's free thinking. In the name of science, which in its form as scientism has the characteristics of a new church, the technocrats have created a new Inquisition against those who have an independent mind. The Great Reset aims to put into general operation the mechanisms of control prepared in the Corona health dictatorship. A spirit of lies and fear is at work in it, a spirit which was formerly spread by the Inquisition.

This spirit of lies and fear paralyzes people's sense of freedom and produces a technological and materialistic culture in which transhumanism is the new ideology. In medicine, it stimulates symptom control by chemical means instead of supporting the constructive and healing powers of the human body, soul, and spirit. It also encourages artificially stimulating the immune system with vaccinations instead of going through illness in a controlled way to build up immunity, in a healthy life in harmony with nature. This spirit acts as an illegitimate *zeitgeist* or "spirit of the age" that wants to bring the whole world under its influence.

That spirit had a name in the ancient cultures. The ancient Iranians called him Ahriman, the Egyptians Seth or Set, the Israelites Satan, the Muslims Sheytan, the Germanic tribes the Fenris Wolf and the early Christians the "Illegitimate Prince of this World." In our culture he operates through fear and in a form of thinking that denies the spiritual essence and ideals of human beings and recognises only the laws of matter.

According to various spiritual traditions, a legitimate *zeitgeist* has been at work in our time since the end of the 19th century, inspiring people to live out of their moral ideals, to think spiritually with head and heart, and to fight courageously for a world of love, wisdom, and truth. In the Judeo-Christian tradition, this *zeitgeist* is the archangel Michael, who is the face of God. This spiritual thinking is not intellectual, abstract, and immoral, like that of the technocrats, but rather creative, warm-hearted, moral, open to spiritual inspirations and oriented towards the good of all people. When this thinking blossoms, we can free ourselves from the technocratic plans of the elites that are being prepared in the Great Reset. When we begin to think in that way, a spiritual culture that restores human dignity, heals our sick societies, and reconnects us with nature becomes possible. The decision to take action to create such a possible culture is the responsibility of every one of us.